Robert Williams Buchanan

Balder the Beautiful

A Song of Divine Death

Robert Williams Buchanan

Balder the Beautiful
A Song of Divine Death

ISBN/EAN: 9783337779610

Printed in Europe, USA, Canada, Australia, Japan

Cover: Foto ©Lupo / pixelio.de

More available books at **www.hansebooks.com**

BALDER THE BEAUTIFUL

𝔄 𝔖𝔬𝔫𝔤 𝔬𝔣 𝔇𝔦𝔳𝔦𝔫𝔢 𝔇𝔢𝔞𝔱𝔥

By ROBERT BUCHANAN

ὦ Θάνατε παιάν !

"For as in Adam all die, even so in Christ shall all be made alive. . . . But some man will say, How are the dead raised up? and with what body do they come? Thou fool, that which thou sowest is not quickened, except it die. . . . Behold, I show you a mystery; we shall not all sleep, but we shall all be changed."—PAUL, COR. 1st Ep. chap. xv

.WILLIAM MULLAN & SON

34 PATERNOSTER ROW LONDON

4 DONEGAL PLACE BELFAST

1877

CONTENTS.

P R O E M   T O——

A SONG OF A DREAM.

O WHAT is this cry in our burning ears,

　　And what is this light on our eyes, dear love ?

The cry is the cry of the rolling years,

　　As they break on the sun-rock, far above ;

And the light is the light of that rock of gold

　　As it burneth bright in a starry sea ;

And the cry is clearer a hundredfold,

　　And the light more bright, when I gaze on thee.

· My weak eyes dazzle beneath that gleam,

　　My sad ears deafen to hear that cry :

I was born in a dream, and I dwell in a dream,

　　And I go in a dream to die !

O whose is this hand on my forehead bare,

　　And whose are these eyes that look in mine ?

· The hand is the Earth's soft hand of air,

　　The eyes are the Earth's—thro' tears they shine ;

And the touch of the band is so soft, so light,

　　As the ray of the blind orbs blesseth me ;

But the touch is softest, the eyes most bright,

    When I sit and smile by the side of thee.

For the mortal Mother's blind eyes beam

    With the long-lost love of a life gone by,

On her breast I woke in a beauteous dream,

    And I go in a dream to die !

O what are these voices around my way,

    And what are these shadows that stir below ?

The voices of waifs in a world astray,

    The shadows of souls that come and go.

And I hear and see, and I wonder more,

    For their features are fair and strange as mine,

But most I wonder when most I pore

    On the passionate peace of this face of thine.

We walk in silence by wood and stream,

    Our gaze upturned to the same blue sky :

We move in a dream, and we love in a dream,

    And we go in our dream to die !

O what is this music of merry bells,

    And what is this laughter across the wold ?

'Tis the mirth of a market that buys and sells,

    'Tis the laughter of men that are counting gold.

I walk thro' Cities of silent stone,

    And the public places alive I see ;

The wicked flourish, the weary groan,

    And I think it real, till I turn to thee !

And I smile to answer thine eyes' bright beam,
    For I know all's vision that darkens by :
That they buy in a dream, and they sell in a dream,
    And they go in a dream to die.

O what are these shapes on their thrones of gold,
    And what are those clouds around their feet ?
The shapes are kings with their hearts clay-cold,
    The clouds are armies that ever meet ;
I see the flame of the crimson fire,
    I hear the murdered who moan "Ah me !"—
My bosom aches with its bitter ire,
    And I think it real, till I turn to thee !
And I hear thee whisper, "These shapes but seem—
    They are but visions that flash and fly,
While we move in a dream, and love in a dream,
    And go in our dream to die !"

O what are these Spirits that o'er us creep,
    And touch our eyelids and drink our breath
The first, with a flower in his hand, is Sleep ;
    The next, with a star on his brow, is Death.
We fade before them whene'er they come,
    (And never single those spirits be !)
A little season my lips are dumb,
    But I waken ever,—and look for thee.

Yea ever each night when the pale stars gleam

    And the mystical Brethren pass me by,

This cloud of a trance comes across my dream,

    As I seem in my dream to die !

O what is this grass beneath our feet,

    And what are these beautiful under-blooms?

The grass is the grass of the churchyard, Sweet,

    The flowers are flowers on the quiet tombs.

I pluck them softly, and bless the dead,

    Silently o'er them I bend the knee,

But my tendèrest blessing is surely said,

    Tho' my tears fall fast, when I turn to thee.

For our lips are tuned to the same sad theme,

    We think of the loveless dead, and sigh ;

Dark is the shadow across our dream,

    For we go in that dream to die !

O what is this moaning so faint and low,

    And what is this crying from night to morn?

The moaning is that of the souls that go,

    The crying is that of the souls new-born.

The life-sea gathers with stormy calls,

    The wind blows shrilly, the foam flies free,

The great wave rises, the great wave falls,

    I swim to its height by the side of thee !

With arms outstretching and throats that scream,
  With faces that flash into foam and fly,
Our beings break in the light of a dream,
  As the great waves gather and die !

O what is this Spirit with silvern feet,
  His bright head wrapt in a saffron veil ?
Around his raiment our wild arms beat,
  We cling unto them, but faint and fail.
'Tis the Spirit that sits on the twilight star,
  And soft to the sound of the waves sings he,
He leads the chaunt from his crystal car,
  And I join in the mystical chaunt with thee,
And our beings burn with the heavenly theme,
  For he sings of wonders beyond the sky,
Of a god-like dream, and of gods in a dream,
  Of a dream that cannot die !

O closer creep to this breast of mine ;
  We rise, we mingle, we break, dear love !
A space on the crest of the wave we shine,
  With light and music and mirth we move;
Before and behind us (fear not, sweet !)
  Blackens the trough of the surging sea—
A little moment our mouths may meet,
  A little moment I cling to thee ;

Onward the wonderful waters stream,

'Tis vain to struggle, 'tis vain to cry—

We wake in a dream, and we ache in a dream,

And we break in a dream, and die!

But who is this other with hair of flame,

The naked feet, and the robe of white?

A Spirit too, with a sweeter name,

A softer smile, a serener light.

He wraps us both in a golden cloud,

He thrills our frames with a fire divine,

Our souls are mingled, our hearts beat loud,

My breath and being are blent with thine;

And the sun-rock flames with a flash supreme,

And the starry waves have a stranger cry—

We climb to the crest of our golden dream,

For we dream that we cannot die!

Aye! the cry rings loud in our burning ears,

And the light flames bright on our eyes, dear love,

And we know the cry of the rolling years

As they break on the sun-rock far above;

And we know the light of the rock of gold,

As it burneth bright in a starry sea,

And the glory deepens a thousandfold

As I name the immortal gods and thee!

We shrink together beneath that gleam,

    We cling together before that cry ;

We were made in a dream, and we fade in a dream,

    And if death be a dream, we die !

BALDER THE BEAUTIFUL.

The gods are brethren.   Wheresoe'er
They set their shrines of love or fear,
In Grecian woods, by banks of Nile,
Where cold snows sleep or roses smile,
The gods are brethren.   Zeus the Sire
Was fashion'd of the self-same fire
As Odin ; He whom Ind brought forth
Hath his pale kinsmen east and north ;
And more than one since life began
Hath known Christ's agony for Man.
The gods are brethren.   Kin by fate,
In gentleness as well as hate,
'Mid heights that only Thought may climb
_   They come, they go ; they are, or seem ;_
Each, rainbow'd from the rack of Time,
_   Casts broken lights across God's Dream._

I.

THE BIRTH OF BALDER.

THE BIRTH OF BALDER.

I.

BALDER'S BIRTH-SONG.

THERE blent with his growing
The leaf and the flower,
The wind lightly blowing
Its balm from afar,
The smile of the sunshine,
The sob of the shower,
The beam of the moonshine,
The gleam of the star.
'Mid shining of faces
And waving of wings,
With gifts from all places
Came beautiful things ;

The blush from the blossom,
  The bloom from the corn,
Blent into his bosom,
  Ere Balder was born.

As a rainbow in heaven
  Was woven the rune,
The colours were seven
    Most dim and divine;
Thro' regions of thunder
  Serene swam the moon,
With white rays of wonder
    Completing the sign.
The snow-star was gleaming
  Cold, silent, and clear,
Its bright image beaming
    Deep down in the mere;
The night grew profounder,
  The earth slept forlorn,
With the drift wrapt around her
    Ere Balder was born.

Beside a waste water
  Lay Frea alone,
In Asgard they sought her,
  To earth she had crept;
The Father was sitting
  Snow-white on his throne,
The night-clouds were flitting,
  The wind-harps were swept.
No eyes divine found her—
  She lay as one dead—
Vast forests around her,
  Black vapours o'erhead,—
She saw not,—she heard not—
  But weary and worn,
Snow-shrouded, she stirred not,
  Ere Balder was born.

There, hid from the Father,
  She brooded below,
In realms where pines gather
  Ice-robed and ice-crown'd,

And the great trees were drooping,
  Struck down by the snow,
With chilly arms stooping
    To touch the white ground.
While whirlwinds were weaving
    Their raiment of cloud,
She sat there conceiving,
    Dark, brooding, and bow'd ;
But where the boughs thicken'd
    A bird sang one morn,—
And she kindled and quicken'd,
    Ere Balder was born.

Then by that great water,
    Within the dark woods,
The dawn broke, and brought her
    A glimmer of Spring !
The gray geese came crying
    Far over the floods,
The black crane pass'd, flying
    With slow waft of wing.

And when the moon's silver
  Was shed on the mere,
The cry of the culver
  Was heard far and near,
And the owls to each other
  Made answers forlorn,—
And she smiled, the sad Mother,
  Ere Balder was born.

Then the peace and the splendour
  Of powers of the night,
And the strength that grows tender
  Where dusk rivers run,
The beam of the moonshine,
  The soft starry light,
And the first smile of sunshine,
  Were woven in one.
And they mingled within her
  With motions of earth
To strengthen and win her
  To mystical birth ;—

By the pangs of a woman
  The goddess was torn,
Ere, with heart of the human,
  God Balder was born.

The wind-gods were blowing
  Their trumpets of might,
The skies were still snowing,
  And dark was the wold,—
With a rock for her pillow
  Lay Frea that night,
Beneath a great willow
  All leafless and cold—
But the earth to strange motion
  Was stirring around,
And the ice of the ocean
  Had split with shrill sound ;—
When coldly upspringing
  Arose the red morn,
To a sound as of singing
  Bright Balder was born !

His hair was as golden
  As lily-hearts be,
When, softly unfolden,
    From black tarns they rise,—
The lights of the azure,
  The shades of the sea,
Blent into the pleasure
    Of beautiful eyes ;
Like the aspen that lingers
  Where waters run fleet
Was the touch of his fingers
  The thrill of his feet ;
White, white as the blossom
  That blows on the thorn,
On Frea's fair bosom
  Bright Balder was born.

While soften'd and sadden'd
  With love shone her face,
Uplooking he gladden'd
    And clung to her breast,

For a light as of summer
  Swept over the place,
When the shining new-comer
  Awoke from his rest !
And the willow and alder
  Thrill'd out unto bloom,
And the lilac brought Balder
  Its light and perfume,
While the merle sable-suited
  Sang merry by morn,
And with bill of gold fluted
  That Balder was born !

At the notes of the singer
  The sun glimmer'd gay,
And touch'd with bright finger
  The child as he stirred !
For the snow from the mountains
  Was melting away,
And the sound of the fountains
  Upleaping was heard ;

And the black soil was broken
  To radiance of flowers,
While the Bow for a token
  Gleam'd down thro' the showers ;
Deep under the fallow
  Now sprouted the corn,
And swift flash'd the swallow,
  For Balder was born!

Yea, again up in heaven
  Was rainbow'd the rune,
And the colours were seven
  Most dim and divine :
Sweet creatures work'd under
  The sun and the moon,
Completing the wonder
  With whisper and sign.
With eyes brightly gleaming
  The squirrel came near,
In flocks swam the lemming
  Across the great mere,

And the gold-speckled spider
Found Frea that morn,
And was busy beside her
When Balder was born.

And with him came waking
The leaf and the flower,
The wind lightly shaking
Its balm from afar,
The smile of the sunshine,
The sob of the shower,
The beam of the moonshine,
The gleam of the star.
'Mid shining of faces
And waving of wings,
With gifts from all places
Came beautiful things;
By night-time and day-time
No life was forlorn,
'Twas leaf-time, 'twas May-time,
And Balder was born.

Yet the spell had been woven

   Long ages ago,

That the clouds should be cloven,

   The Father undone,

When the light of the sunshine,

   The white of the snow,

And the starshine and moonshine,

   Were mingled in one ;

When the wind and the water,

   The star and the flower,

Found a goddess, and brought her

   Their strength for a dower ;

Yea, in runes it was written,

   With letters forlorn,

That the gods should be smitten

   When Balder was born.

Then roar'd the mad thunder

   From regions afar,

And the world darken'd under

   That wrath of the skies,

But the new-born, upleaping
As bright as a star,
Awoke from his sleeping
With love in his eyes ;—
And the dark rain ceased falling,
With slow silvern thrills,
And the cuckoo came, calling
Aloud on the hills,
And the glad Earth uplifted
Her face to the morn,
And past the storm drifted,
For Balder was born.

. . . In the sedge of the river
The swan makes its nest ;
In the mere, with no quiver,
Stands shadow'd the crane ;
Earth happy and still is,
Peace dwells in her breast,
And the lips of her lilies
Drink balm from the rain ;

The lamb in the meadow

  Upsprings with no care,

Deep in the wood's shadow

  Is born the young bear ;

The ash and the alder,

  The flowers and the corn,

All waited for Balder,—

  And Balder is born !

II.

HIS GROWTH AND GODHEAD.

LOVELY as light and blossoms are,
  And gentle as the dew,
A white god stainless as a star,
  Deep-hidden, Balder grew.

For in the time when violets grow,
  And birds sing thro' the showers,
Pale Frea left her child below,
  Upon a bank of flowers.

And heavenward now on weary feet
  The mighty goddess flies,
And kneeleth at the Father's seat,
  And gazeth in his eyes.

Around her in those shadowy halls
  The great gods darkly tread.

" Where is thy child ? " each cold voice calls ;
　Calmly she answereth, " Dead.

" The arrows of the gods are keen,
　An infant's heart is mild ;
Buried within the forest green,
　Now slumbereth my child.

" The robin strew'd him o'er with leaves,
　And closed his eyes of blue,
And overhead the spider weaves
　Her rune of silk and dew."

Pale at the mighty banquet board
　The Mother sat in pain :
The great gods smiling, with no word,
　Drank deep, and breathed again . . .

But down within the forest dim
　The child divine lies quick !
The slanted sunlight comes to him
　Thro' branches woven thick.

He drinks no nurture of the breast,
  No mother's kiss he knows;
Warm as a song bird in its nest
  He feels the light, and grows.

Around him flock all gentle things
  Which range the forest free :
Each shape that blooms, each shape that sings,
  Looks on him silently.

The light is melted on his lips
  And on his eyes of blue,
And from the shining leaves he sips
  The sweetness of the dew.

And slowly like an earthborn child
  He learns to walk and run—
A forest form, with laughter wild,
  He wanders in the sun.

And now he knows the great brown bear,
  And sitteth with its young,

And of their honey takes his share,
  Sucking with thirsty tongue.

Around him as he comes and goes
  There clings a golden mist,
And in his bright hair blooms a rose,
  And a bird sings on his wrist !

And wheresoe'er he sets his feet
  Fair ferns and flowers spring,
And honeysuckles scented sweet
  Grow where his fingers cling.

He calls, and wood-doves at the cry
  Come down to be caress'd ;
Curl'd in his arms the lynx will lie,
  Its lips against his breast.

O look into his happy eyes,
  As lustrous as the dew !
A light like running water lies
  Within their depths of blue ;

And there the white cloud's shadow dim
  Stirs, mirror'd soft and gray,
And far within the dream-dews swim
  With melancholy ray.

Ev'n thus in beauteous shape he grows,
  Unknown, unseen, unheard,
And night by night he takes repose
  Like any flower or bird.

He drinks the balmy breath of Earth,
  He feels the light and rain,
Till, like a thing of mortal birth,
  He shares her peace or pain.

A wild white shape with wondering eyes
  He walks by wood and stream,
And softly on his spirit lies
  The burthen of a dream.

His hair is like the midnight sun's,
  All golden-red and bright;

But radiance as of moonrise runs
  Upon his limbs of white.

And now the wood without a sound
  Hushes its leaves in dread:
Beauty and mystery surround
  The silence of his tread.

Quietly as a moonbeam creeps
  He moves from place to place ;
Soft steals the starlight, as he sleeps,
  To breathe upon his face.

The ground grows green beneath his feet,
  While, trembling on the stem,
The pale flowers drink again, full sweet,
  The breath he draws from them.

Now brightly gleams the soft green sod,
  The golden seeds are sown ;
O pale white lily of a god,
  Thou standest now full blown !

II.

THE FINDING OF BALDER.

THE FINDING OF BALDER.

I.

FREA IN THE WOOD.

BLUE night.   Along the lonely forest way
The goddess, mighty-limb'd and marble white,
Tall in the shadow of the pines that waved
Their black arms in the moonrise overhead,
Stole silent-footed.   Round her naked feet
The dews were luminous, and the breath of flowers
Rose from the scented path of grass and fern,
And all was stiller than a maiden's dream.

From grove to grove she went, like one that knew
Each shadow of that silent forest old,
And ever as she went the tangled light
That trembled on her thro' the woven boughs
Grew deeper and more dewy, until at last

She knew by chilly gleams upon the grass

That dawn was come. Still did that umbrage deep

Remain in dimness, tho' afar away

The hills were kindling with dull blood-red fires;

But when the trumpet of the day was blown

From the great golden gateways of the sun,

When leaf by leaf the crimson rose o' the east

Open'd, and leaf by leaf illumed in turn

Glitter'd the snowy lily of the north,

She left the shelter of those woods, and stood

Under the shining canopy of heaven.

Before her lay a vast and tranquil lake,

And wading in its shallows silently

Great storks of golden white and light green cranes

Stood sentinel, while far as eye could see,

Swam the wild water-lily's oilëd leaves.

Still was that place as sleep, yet evermore

A stir amid its stillness ; for behold,

At every breath of the warm summer wind

Blown on the beating bosom of the lake,

The white swarms of the new-born lily-flowers,

A pinch of gold-dust in the heart of each,

Rose from the bubbling depths, and open'd up,

And floated luminous with cups of snow.

Across that water came so sweet an air,

It fell upon the immortal mother's brow

Like coolest morning dew, and tho' she stood

Beneath the open arch of heaven, the light

Stole thro' the gauze of a soft summer mist

Most gentle and subdued.   Then while she paused

Close to the rippling shallows sown with reeds,

Those cranes and storks arose above her head

In one vast cloud of flying green and gold;

And from the under-heaven innumerable

The lilies upward to the surface snow'd,

Till all the waters glitter'd gold and white;

And lo! the sun swept shining up the east,

And thro' the cloud of birds, and on the lake,

Shot sudden rays of light miraculous,—

Until the goddess veil'd her dazzled eyes,

And with the heaving whiteness at her feet

Her bosom heaved, till of that tremulous life

She seem'd a throbbing part!

Tall by the marge

The goddess tower'd, and her immortal face

Was shining as anointed ; then she cried,

" Balder ! " and like the faint cry of a bird

That passeth overhead, the sound was borne

Between the burning ether and the earth.

Then once again she called, outstretching arms,

" Balder ! "   Upon her face the summer light

Trembled in benediction, while the voice

Was lifted up and echoed till it died

Far off amid the forest silences.

A space she paused, smiling and listening,

Gazing upon the lilies as they rose

Large, luminously fair, and new-baptized ;

And once again she would have call'd aloud,

When far across the waters suddenly

There shone a light as of the morning star ;

Which coming nearer seem'd as some bright bird

Floating amid the lilies and their leaves,

And presently, approaching closer still,

Assumed the likeness of a shining shape,

Who, with white shoulders from the waters reaching,

And sunlight burning on his golden hair,

Swam like a swan. Upon his naked arms

The amber light was melted, while they clove

The crystal depths and softly swept aside

The glittering lilies and their clustering leaves ;

And on the forehead of him burnt serene

A light as of a pearl more wonderful

Than ever from the crimson seas of Ind

Was snatch'd by human hand ; for pearl it seem'd,

Tho' blood-red, and as lustrous as a star.

Him Frea breathless watch'd, for all the air

Was golden with his glory as he came ;

And o'er his head the bird-cloud hover'd bright

With murmurs deep ; and thro' the lake he swam

With arm-sweeps swift, till in the shallows bright,

Still dripping from the kisses of the waves,

He rose erect in loveliness divine.

The lustre from his ivory arms and limbs

Stream'd as he stood, and from his yellow hair

A glory rain'd upon his neck and breast,

While burning unextinguish'd on his brow
Shone that strange star.

               Then as he shining rose,
And on her form the new effulgence fell,
The goddess, with her face beatified,
Yet gentle as a mortal mother's, cried
" Balder ! my Balder ! "—and while from all the
    woods,
And from the waters wide, and from the air
Still rainbow'd with the flashing flight of birds,
Innumerable echoes answer'd, " Balder ! "—
Clad in his gentle godhead Balder stood,
Bright, beautiful, and palpably divine.

II.

THE SHADOW IN THE WOOD.

" MOTHER ! " he said, and on that mother's face

Fixing the brightness of his starry eyes,

He kiss'd her, smiling.   E'en as sunlight falls

Upon the whiteness of some western cloud,

Irradiating and illuming it,

His beauty smote her sadness : silently

She trembled ; and her large immortal orbs

Were raised to heaven.   For a space she stood

O'er-master'd by that splendour, but at last,

While softly from her forehead and her cheeks

The loving rapture ebb'd, and once again

Her face grew alabaster calm and cold,

Her soul found speech.

"O Balder ! best beloved !

God of the sunlight and the summer stars,

White Shepherd of the gentle beasts and birds,

Benign-eyed watcher of all beauteous things,

Thou know'st me! thou rememberest! thou art here,

Supreme, a god, my Son!—Within thine eyes

Immortal innocence and mortal peace

Are blent to love and gentleness divine;

And tho' I left thee in these woods a babe,

Fair and unconscious as a fallen flower,

And tho' I have not watch'd thy beauty grow,

I come again to seek thee, and behold

Thou know'st me—thou rememberest! thou art here,

Supreme, a god, my Son!   Blest be those powers

To whose lone keeping I committed thee!

The heavens have shone upon thee, and the boughs

Have curtain'd thee for slumber, and the rain

Hath smooth'd thy soft limbs with its silvern fingers,

And gently ministrant to thee have been

The starlight and the moonlight and the dew,

And in their seasons all the forest flowers;

And from the crimson of divine deep dawns

And from the flush of setting suns, thy cheeks

Have gather'd such a splendour as appals

The vision, even mine.   Balder! beloved!

Speak to me ! tell me how thy soul hath fared
Alone so long in these green solitudes."

She ceased, and Balder smiled again, and took
Her hand and held it as he answer'd her ;
And ne'er was sound of falling summer showers
On boughs with lilac laden and with rose,
Or cuckoo-cries o'er emerald uplands heard,
Or musical murmurs of dark summer dawns,
More sweet than Balder's voice. " O Mother, Mother,"
It answer'd, " when I saw thee from afar,
Silent, stone-still, with shadow at thy feet,
I knew thee well, for nightly evermore
I have seen thy shape in sleep." And while the face
Of the great goddess kindled once again
With its maternal love ineffable,
He added, " Thou shalt read me all my dream !
For in a dream here have I grown and thriven,
With such dim rapture as those lilies feel
Awakening and uprising mystically
From darkness to the brightness of the air ;

And growing in a dream I have beheld

All things grow gladder with me, sun and star,

Strange fronds, and all the wonders of the wood;

Till round me, with me, soul and part of me,

This world hath kindled like an opening rose.

And happy had I been as any bird

Singing full-throated in the summer light,

But for some dark and broken images

Which come to me in sleep—yea come each night

When from the starlight and the silvern moon

I fade with closèd eyes.   But thou art here,

And in the love of thy celestial looks

I read the answer to the mystery

Of my dim earthly being."

As he spake,

Across the goddess' face and thro' her frame

There pass'd the wind of an old prophecy,

Bending her downward as a storm-swept bough.

" In sleep ! what shapes have come to thee in sleep?"

She cried, and Balder answer'd, " It were long

To tell thee all, my Mother ! but meseems

I have dream'd nightly of mysterious forms

White-brow'd like thee and very beautiful—

Strange spirits, each more bright than is a star,

In robes of linen and of whitest wool,

And some all raimentless as leaf or flower,

And in their nakedness the more divine."

Then Frea smiled and answer'd, " That is well—

These, Balder, are thy sisters and my kin,

Less beautiful than thou, yet very fair."

And Balder said, " Ofttimes mine eyes have seen

Great shapes caparison'd in burning gold,

Tall as the tallest pine within these woods,

Who flash'd red brands together, or upheld

Bright cups of ruby, gazing on each other ! "

And Frea smiled and said, " That too is well—

Those, Balder, are thy brethren and thy peers,

Great gods, yet less than thou."   Then Balder's voice

Sank lower, saying, " Three times in my sleep

I have seen my Father ! "

                    Frea's cheek was blanch'd,

And pressing one white hand upon her heart,

" How seem'd he in thy sleep ? " the goddess sigh'd,

" Frown'd he or smiled he ? speak ! " And Balder
    said,

In solemn whispers, sinking ever lower,

" My soul perceived a darkness and a sound

Of many voices wailing, and I seem'd

As one that drifts upon a sunless water,

Amid the washing of a weary rain—

Wet were my locks and dripping, and my limbs

Hung heavily as lead—while wave by wave

I floated to some vapour-shrouded shore.

At last, wash'd in upon the slippery weeds,

I saw before me on a mountain top

One brooding like a cloud ; and as a cloud

At first he seem'd, yet ever as I look'd

Grew shapen to an image terrible,

With eyes eternal gazing down at mine.

And as I rose a voice came from the cloud

Like far-off muffled thunder, crying, ' Balder !

Come hither, my son Balder ! '—when in fear

I scream'd and woke, and saw the daylight dance

Golden upon the forests and the meres."

He ceased; and utter pity fill'd his soul
To see across his beauteous Mother's face
The scorching of unutterable pain;
Then thrice the troubled goddess raised her eyes
And gazed up northward where the rose-red shafts
Of dawn were trembling on the cloud-capt towers
Of Asgard; thrice the sorrow master'd her;
But soon her strong soul conquer'd, and she forced
A strange sad look of calm. " If that be all,
Take courage—and I do conjure thee now,
Fear not thy Father. If that Father ever
Hath cherish'd dread of thee, the loveliness
Of thy completed godhead shall disarm
His wrath,—yea, win his love." Her gentle hand
Clasp'd his with more than mortal tenderness,
And in his eyes she gazed again and drank
The solace of his beauty while the dawn
Encrimson'd both and all the heavens and air,
But Balder trembled shrinking to her side,
And cried, with quick eyes glancing all around,
" Mother! that is not all!"

"O speak no more,"

The goddess said, " if aught else terrible

Thine eyes have vision'd or thy sense hath dream'd,

Speak, speak, no more ! " but Balder answer'd,

   " Mother !

A weight is on my heart, and I must speak.

Last night I dream'd the strangest dream of dreams !

Methought I in the summer woodland walk'd

And pluck'd white daffodils and pansies blue,

And as I went I sang such songs as sing

The spirits of the forest and the stream ;

And presently the golden light went in,

But balmy darkness follow'd, for the rain

Patter'd with diamond dews innumerable

On the green roof of umbrage overhead.

I stood and waited, listening.   Then methought

I heard a voice from far away—*thy* voice

It seem'd, my Mother—murmur three times 'Balder!'

And as it ceased, there pierced the wood's green heart

A shriek so sharp and shrill that all my blood

Turn'd cold to listen !   Suddenly I felt

My brow was damp with chilly drops of rain,

And looking up I saw that every leaf

Had wither'd from the branches overhead,

Leaving them black against a sunless heaven

Of dark and dreary gray.   Again I heard

Thy voice moan 'Balder,' and methought the
  boughs

Toss'd their wild arms above and echoed ' Balder,'

When lo, the black and miserable rain

Came slower and slower, wavering through the dark,

Till every drop was as a flake of white

Falling upon the ground as light as wool !

And terror seized me, and I felt my heart

Cold as a stone, and from my hands the flowers

Dropt, wither'd, with that whiteness on the ground.

I tried to stir, and could not stir ; I sought

To shake the chilly flakes from off my neck,

But could not ; and each time I sought to cry,

My cries were frozen in my throat.   Now mark !

O mark, my mother, for these things are strange !

As thus I stood, mine eyes were 'ware of ONE,

A Shape with shadowy arms outspread like wings,

Which, hovering o'er me even as a hawk,

Fix'd on my face its fatal luminous eyes.

O Mother, that wan shape ! The forest holds,

In form of beast or bird or glittering snake,

No likeness of its awful lineaments !

For ever as its features seem'd to take

Clearness and semblance, they did fade away

Into a swooning dimness; and it seem'd

Now shapen and now shapeless, blowing amid

The wonder of that wan and sunless shower.

Yet ever as I gazed it gazed again,

And ever circling nearer seem'd in act

To swoop upon me with cold claws and clutch

The heart that flutter'd wildly in my breast.

At last that look became too much to bear :

Answering at last *thy* scream, I scream'd aloud ;

And as I scream'd, I woke—and saw again

The sunlight on the forests and the meres."

Now ev'n as Balder spake the goddess' face

Was like a shrouded woman's ; once again

She gazed at heaven, and her eyes were glazed

With agony and despair, for now she knew
That shape which Balder had beheld in dream
Was he whom mortal men have christen'd Death.
At last she spake, and all her proud soul flash'd,
Rebuking its own terror. "Unto all,
Yea even unto gods upon their thrones,
Such shadows come in sleep ; thy Father even
Hath had his visions, and I too have mine ;
But be of comfort since thou art my Son,
For he who hover'd o'er thee in thy dream
Is impotent against the strength of gods.
Haunter is he of this sad nether sphere,
And on the little life of bird and beast,
And on the life of flowers and falling leaves,
His breath comes chill, but to the Shapes divine
He is as wind that bloweth afar below
The silence of the peaks."

        Ev'n as she spake,
On her bright Balder gazed not, but with eyes
Fix'd as in fascination, cried aloud
"*Look ! look !*"—and pointed.

Close to that bright spot
Whereon they stood in the full flame of day,
The forest open'd, flashing green and gold,
Sparkling with quick and rapturous thrill of leaves
And rainbow-flush of flowers.   Upon a bough
That reach'd its heavy-laden emerald arm
Into the summer light beyond the shade,
There clung, with panting breast and fluttering wings,
A trembling ringdove whose soft iris'd eyes
Were fix'd like Balder's on some shape of dread
Just visible in the shadow, lying low
Under the scented umbrage of the wood.
A Form, yet indistinct as the green sheen ;
A Face, yet featureless ; a head with eyes
Now faint as drops of dew, now strangely bright
As lustrous gems.   Crouch'd on the under-grass,
It watch'd in serpent fashion every thrill
Of that bright bird ; while all around, the air
Was mad and merry with the summer song
Of choirs that sat alive on leafy boughs,
Singing aloud !

Then came a hush, wherein

Every faint pulse of life in those great woods

Was heard to beat; and then the fated bird

Cooing and quivering fluttered from the bough,

And 'mid the summer sheen beyond the shade,

With one last dying tremor of the wings,

Lay stricken still. . . . Among the darkening leaves

There was a stir, as creeping thro' the gloom,

Scarce visible, fixing eyes on that dead dove,

Forth from his lair the form began to crawl.

And Balder sicken'd, and his sense grew cold.

But with a queenly gesture Frea rose,

And pointed with her white imperious hand

Into the forest.   Suddenly the shape

Was 'ware of that pale goddess and her son

More beauteous and insufferably bright.

A moment in the dimness of his lair

He paused, uprearing, as in act to spring,

A head half human, with a serpent's eyes;

Then, conscious of some presence that he feared,

All swift and silent, like a startled snake,

He faded back into the shadowy woods.

III.

FULL GODHEAD.

O WHITHER are they wending side by side
    Thro' that green forest wide ?
Down the deep dingles, amid ferns and flowers,
    They wander hours and hours.
Bright-lock'd, with limbs of alabaster white,
    Now gleaming in the light,
Now 'mong the dusky umbrage of the glade
    Deep'ning to amber shade,
Their eyes on one another, whither away
    Do these Immortals stray ?

She murmurs, " Thou shalt mark all things that be ;
    The rivers and the sea,
The mountains that for ever crimson'd lie
    Against the arctic sky,

The meteors that across the pale pole flit,

  Strangely illuming it;

And thou shalt look on gods, thy kin and mine,

  Since *thou* too art divine."

Divine !—The forest glimmers where he goes

  To crimson and to rose!

And wheresoe'er he comes no creature fears;

  Each lingers, sees, and hears.

The boughs bend down to touch his yellow hair;

  Around his white feet bare

The grass waves amorous; on his shoulder white

  The singing birds alight,

Singing the sweeter; and in spaces clear

  The brown-eyed dappled deer

With tremulous ear and tail around him stand,

  Licking his outstretch'd hand

With warm rough tongues. He sings—all things around

  Are husht to hear the sound!

He smiles—all things are smiling—wood and stream

  With some new glory gleam,

Dark branches blossom, and the greensward nigh

  Is sunnier than the sky!

She murmurs, " They have cherish'd thee indeed,
　　In answer to thy need.
Ere thou wast born, into thy veins they grew,
　　Earth, sunlight, air, and dew,
The flower, the leaf, star's glimmer and bird's song;
　　And these have made thee strong
With other strength than ours; for ne'er till now,
　　On any immortal brow
Have I beheld such living splendour shine
　　As lies this hour on thine.
O sunbeam of the gods ! O fairer far
　　Than ev'n Immortals are !
Divinest, gentlest, by the glad Earth given
　　To be a lamp in heaven ! "
Divine !—The boughs shook down their shafts of green
　　And gleam'd to golden sheen;
The silvern snake stole from the dark tree-root
　　And twined round Balder's foot
With happy eyes; the tiger-moth and bee
　　About him hover'd free;
With yellow aureole his head was crown'd,
　　And his bright body around

There swam a robe of sunshine scented sweet,

    Clothing him head to feet.

She crieth, " Could the Father see thee there,

    While on thy silken hair

The soft light trembles like a shining hand !

    Couldst thou before him stand,

Flowers round thy feet, a dove upon thy wrist,

    Earth-blest and heaven-kist,

Would he not smile? would he not scorn full soon

    The wearily woven rune

Which said that sorrow should be born when *thou*

    Didst break with orient brow

The night-cloud of the Earth ?   O Son ! my Son !

    The crimson thread is spun,

The snow-white bud is blown, and now, behold !

    The branch with fruit of gold

Hath grown full straight and swings i' the summer
    shine

    Ineffably divine."

He questions, "Whither go we?" She replies,
    " To that dim Land which lies
Ev'n as a cloud around the Father's feet!"
    He smiles, his pulses beat
With brighter rapture. "Shall mine eyes then see
    My Father?" crieth he;
" Where dwells he? and my brethren, where dwell
    they?"
    She answereth, " Far away!"
Then, her face darken'd by some dreamy dread,
    She moves with sadder tread.

The shadows grow around them as they stray
    From glade to glade ; their way
Winds still 'mong flowers and leaves, where day and
    night,
    Both sleepless and both bright,
One golden and one silvern, come and go.
    Nor, when dark twilights sow
Their asphodels in the broad fields of blue,
    And a cold summer dew

Gleams on the grass, and moths with fiery eyes
  Flit, and the night-jar cries,
Doth Balder glimmer less divine. Ah, nay !
  Dim things that know not day
Find him and love him; drinking his pure breath
  The white owl hovereth;
About his footprints in the faint moon-ray
  Wild lynxes leap and play;
The ringdoves on the branches brood; meek hares
  Creep from their grassy lairs
To look upon him.   So he goeth by
  Of all things that descry
Beloved, and missed; around him like a veil
  The moonbeams cluster pale,
And all the eyes of heaven with soft dews swim,
  As they gaze down on him.

But now they leave the mighty woods, and pass
  Thro' valleys of deep grass,
Sprinkled with saxifrage and tormentil;
  And many a mountain rill

Leaps by them, singing.   Far away, on high,
    They mark against the sky
Blue-shadow'd mountains crown'd with sparkling snow;
    And thitherward they go.

Thro' lonely mountain valleys in whose breast
    The white grouse makes its nest,
And where in circles wheel the goshawk keen
    And fleet-wing'd peregrine;
Past torrents gashing the dark heathery height
    With gleams of hoary white,
Their shining feet now fall, and where they fare
    Faint rainbows fill the air
And span the streams; with sound of rippling rain
    The cataracts leap amain,
The deer cry from the heights, and all around
    Is full of summer sound.

Silent, upon the topmost peak they come,
    By precipices dumb

And melancholy rocks girt round ; and so

    They reach the realms of snow.

Far o'er their heads a hooded eagle wings

    In ever-widening rings,

Till in the blinding glory of the day

    A speck he fades away.

Then Balder's eyes gaze down. Stretch'd far beneath,

    Forest and field and heath,

Netted with silvern threads of springs and streams,

    Shine in the summer beams—

And valley after valley farther on

    Fades dim into the sun.

He crieth, " Far away methinks I mark

    A mighty Forest dark,

Crown'd by a crimson mist; yonder it lies,

    Stretching into the skies,

And farther than its darkness nought I see."

    And softly answereth she,

" O Balder ! 'tis the Ocean. Vast and strange,

    It changeth without change,

Washing with weary waves for evermore
    The dark Earth's silent shore."
And Balder spake not, but he gazed again
    Thro' the soft mist of rain
Which curtain'd that new wonder from his sight.

    At last, when day and night
Have passed, they cross a purple cape and stand
    On shores of golden sand,
And pausing silent, see beneath the sky
    The mighty Ocean lie.

IV.

THE MAN BY THE OCEAN.

CALMLY it lieth, limitless and deep,
    In windless summer sleep,
And from its fringe, cream-white and set with shells,
    A drowsy murmur swells,
While in its shallows, on its yellow sands,
    Smiling, uplifting hands,
Moves Balder, beckoning with bright looks and words
    The snow-white ocean-birds.
He smiles—the heavens smile answer! All the sea
    Is glistering glassily.
Far out, blue-black amid the waters dim,
    Leviathan doth swim,
Spouts fountain-wise, roars loud, then sinking slow,
    Seeks the green depths below.
All silent. All things sleeping in the light,
    And all most calmly bright!

He walks the weed-strewn strand, and where the waves
    Creep into granite caves,
Green-paven, silver-fretted, roof'd with rose, ·
    He like a sunbeam goes,
And ocean-creatures know him.   The black seal
    Out of the darkness steal
With gentle bleat, or with their lambs arise,
    Their dark and dewy eyes
Uplooking into his; the cormorants green,
    Which ranged in black rows preen
Their dusky plumage, at his footstep's sound
    Turn snake-like necks around,
But rise not; o'er his head the white terns fly
    With shrill unceasing cry;
And out of caverns come the rock-doves fleet,
    Alighting at his feet!
Across the waters darts a shaft supreme
    Of strange and heavenly gleam,
That doth his consecrated form enfold
    Like to a robe of gold,—
While all the Ocean gladdeneth anew,
    Stretch'd bright beneath the blue.

But what is this he findeth on his way,

 Here, where the golden ray

Falleth on sands 'neath crimson crags that rise

 Dark 'gainst the great blue skies?

What is this shape that, breathing soft and deep,

 Lies on its side asleep,

Here on the strand where drifted sea-weeds cling?

 Is it some ocean-thing,

Crept from the emerald darkness of the brine

 To bask i' the summer shine?

Is it some gentle monster whose green home

 Lies far below the foam?

Softly he sleeps, while on his closèd eyes

 The summer sunlight lies;

Around his face, that seemeth wildly fair,

 Hang tawny locks of hair,

On dusky shoulders falling loosely down;

 And lo, his cheeks are brown

With kisses of the sun, and round his limbs

 A light like amber swims

Divinely clear; and by his side is thrown

 A spear of walruss-bone,

A bear-skin blanket, and a seal-hide thong ;
　　So sleeps he, brown and strong ;
And nought that lieth upon land or sea
　　Seemeth more strange than he,
Like some wild birth of ocean wash'd to land,
　　And cast upon the sand
With many a drifting weed and waif beside.

　　"O Mother !" Balder cried,
Suddenly falling on his bended knee,
　　"What shape is this I see ?
It sleeps—it breathes—it lives !"　And Frea said,
　　Scarce turning her proud head,
"It is a mortal man not worth thy care !
　　Ev'n as the birds of the air
They are born, they gladden, and they come and go."
　　But Balder, stooping low,
Passing soft fingers o'er the sleeper's side,
　　And smiling sweetly, cried,
"Awake, awake !" and gently from the strand
　　He raised one strong brown hand.

"Hush!" said the pallid goddess, sighing deep,

 " Lest he awake from sleep,

And touch him not, lest from his mortal breath

 Thou knows't the taint of Death."

" Death!" Balder echoed with a quick sharp
 pain;

 And Frea spake again,

" Nought on this nether sphere which foster'd
 thee,

 But drinks mortality;

Fade not the leaf, the lily, and the rose?

 Yea, and the oak-tree knows

Only its season;—in their seasons all

 Are fashion'd, fade, and fall—

Birds on the boughs, and beasts within the brake,

 Yea, ev'n the hawk and snake,

Are born to perish; and this creature shares

 An earthly lot like theirs."

She paused; for suddenly in the bright sun-ray

 God Balder's cheeks grew gray

And sunken—his eyes dim;—a moment's space

 Across his troubled face

Pass'd darkness. Frea quail'd. A moment more,
And that strange shade pass'd o'er,
And Balder's looks again grew beautiful.

O'erhead, as white as wool,
The calm clouds melted in the burning blue ;
Beneath, the great seas grew
Stiller and calmer, while the immortal one
Stood dreaming in the sun,
On that dark sleeper fixing eyes grown bright
With heavenly love and light.

"O come !" the goddess cried, and took his hand.
Along the shining strand
They pass'd, but evermore god Balder's face
Turn'd backward to the place
Where he had left the weary wight asleep.

Then, as beside the Deep
They wander'd slowly onward, Frea told
Strange tales and legends old

Of living men, and how they came to be,

And how they bend the knee

To gods they know not, till beneath the sun

They die, and all is done.

And ever her finger pointed as she spoke

To wreaths of light-blue smoke

Upcurling heavenward o'er the sleeping seas

From fishing villages.

Love in his heart and wonder on his brow,

Bright Balder hearken'd now

In silence. " Far beyond those lonely woods

And these sea-solitudes,

Peopling the dark Earth, living forms like these

Gather as thick as bees :—

Shapen like gods, yet perishable; born

For ever night and morn,

And night and morn for ever vanishing.

An old dark doom doth cling

Around them and all kindred things that bloom

Out of the green world's womb.

Heed them not *thou !*　To gods they are no more
　　　Than singing birds that soar
A little flight, and fall.　Tho' for a space,
　　　Rear'd in a lowly place,
Thou hast known, as mortals know, Earth's shade
　　and shine,
　　　Another lot is thine !—
To sit among the gods, on heights supreme,
　　　Beyond Man's guess or dream ! "

III.

THE HEAVENWARD JOURNEY.

III.

THE HEAVENWARD JOURNEY.

I.

THE GODDESSES.

THERE is a valley by the northern sea,

O'er-shadow'd softly by eternal hills

And canopied by the ethereal blue.

Above it silently for ever gleam

Cold peaks of ice and snow, and over these

The wind goes, and the shadows of the wind;

While far below, the hollows of the vale

Are strewn most deep with heather and with thyme,

And weeping willows hang their silken hair

O'er dusky tarns with summer lilies sown;

And from these tarns smooth tracts of greensward slope

Until they blend with silvern sands that kiss

The foam-white lips of the still sleeping sea.

Into that valley by a secret way,

The goddess guided her immortal son.

Long had they wander'd, o'er the realms of snow,

Thro' forests vast, down desolate ravines ;

And still, where'er they stept, before their feet

A wind of brightness like a river ran,

And rippled softly into grass and flowers,—

So that they walk'd on rainbows with no rain,

And under heaven made heaven beneath their feet.

At last their path wound upward, while again

They trod the white snows of the topmost peaks,

And saw beneath them, faint and far away,

The secret valley : purple woods of pine,

Crags of wild umbrage lit by flashing falls,

Smooth emerald lawns ; and beyond all, the sea.

And lo ! as Balder gazed, that valley fair

Grew fairer—on its sleep his brightness fell

As benediction—and in saffron light

It swam below him like a sunset cloud.

Down from the lonely heights whereon he stood

A snow-white cataract, like a naked god

With plumes of silver plunging from a peak
Into a purple ocean, headlong flash'd;
Then, lost among the dark green pine-tree tops,
Sounded unseen, mingling its far-off voice
With the deep murmur of the wind-swept boughs.
From rocky shelf to shelf, with golden moss
Enwrought and fringëd with dwarf willow trees,
They now descended in the torrent's track,
And plunging swiftly downward found a path
Thro' the cool darkness of the shadowy woods;
But as they went the dusky forest way
Grew brighter, ever flash'd to softer green
The green leaves, and the sward to sunnier hues,
Till from the leafy umbrage they emerged,
And Balder saw a vision fairer far
Than ever poet fabled in a dream.

Beside those waters, on those emerald lawns
Basking in one eternal summer day,
Lay goddesses divine with half-closed eyes
Gazing out seaward on the crimson isles
Sown in the soft haze of the summer deep.

And there they wove white runes to win the hearts
Of gods and men, while o'er their happy heads
Eternity hung steadfast as a star.
Some stretch'd upon the scented greensward lay
Moveless and wonderfully robed in white ;
Some sitting silent by the dusky tarns
Look'd upward, with their faces dim as dream
Some musing stood, their eyes upon the sea,
Their thoughts afar ; and many up and down
Along the quiet greensward paced and mused.
There was no laughter as of maiden voices,
No sound like human singing : all was still—
Still as a heartbeat, silent as a sleep.

But when from the green shadow of the woods
Immortal Balder in his beauty came,
And stood irresolute in light divine
Gazing upon that wonder of white life,
There was a cry of startled handmaidens
Flocking round goddesses most marble pale.
All to their feet had risen, and one supreme

Tall shape with mailëd plates upon her breast,

A skirt blood-red, and in her hand a spear,

Stood, while pale virgins crouch'd around her feet,

Confronting Balder with black eyes of fire.

Lithe was she as a serpent, lithe and tall,

Her dark skin glimmering bronzëd in the sun,

Her eyebrows black drawn down, and as the beam

Of Balder's beauty struck upon her frame,

She raised her spear, and seem'd in act to strike ;

But Frea, coming stately from the shade,

Cried, " Hold !" and Rota (for 'twas she whose soul

Delights in sowing strife 'mong weary men)

Paused frowning, and the virgins at her feet

Look'd up amazed.

   " Whom bring'st thou here ? " she cried—

" What shape is this, with pale blue human eyes,

Yet more than human brightness, venturing

Where never foot of earthborn thing hath fared ? "

And Frea answer'd gently, " Harm him not !

Nor give him chilly greeting, sister mine—

Kin is he to immortal gods and thee—

'Tis Balder ! my son Balder !"   At the word

The wind of that old prophecy arose

And for a moment like a fever'd breath

Faded across those lawns and sleeping pools ;

And blown from group to group of white-robed
　　forms,

From goddess on to goddess, echoed low

The name of " Balder," till it reached the sands,

And on the far-off foam did die away

In low sad echoes of the mighty main.

Then Balder with a heavenly look advancing

Shone on the place, and Rota dropt her spear,

Still darkening, as in wonder and in scorn

She gazed upon him, crying, " Then he lives !

Woe to the race of Asa since he lives !

Why comes he here ? "   And Balder, with a voice

As sweet as fountains falling, made reply,

" I seek my sisters and my kin divine,

And *thou* art of them !" and he reach'd out hands,

Smiling !

As Rota stood irresolute,

Half-angry, half-disarm'd by his sweet eyes,

Another shape most fair and wonderful

In snow-white robe array'd thro' which her limbs

Shone with a rosy and celestial ray,

Cried " Balder !" in a voice so strange and deep

It fell upon the fountains of his heart

Like sudden light; and two serene large eyes

Shone clear as clearest stars before his sight.

"Who speaketh ?" Balder cried, and the deep voice

Made answer, " O thou foster-child of earth,

With eyes like tender harebells, and with flesh

Bright as the body of a mortal man,

Dost thou not know me ?—I am Gefion,

Whose touch could make thee fruitful as a tree

That drops ripe fruit at every kiss o' the wind."

And Balder would have answer'd eagerly,

But Frea now uplifting a white hand

With queenly gesture, raised her voice and said,

" O sisters ! goddesses ! O lilies fair

Blown in the still pools of eternity !

Be silent for a space, and for a space

Gaze on my son whom to your bowers I bring

For benediction; now, behold, he lives,

Immortal as yourselves and beautiful

As any star that in the heaven of heavens

Hangs luminous, a lamp for mortal eyes.

Him in the secret furrows of the Earth

I cast like seed, while far away the storm

Flash'd to a portent, and I wove my rune:

That neither wind nor snow nor any touch

Of god or goddess might disturb his growth

From season unto season, while he rose

Ev'n as a flower from the sweet-soilèd earth.

There came unto his making leaf and flower,

The soft rain and the shadow of the rain,

The sundew and the moondew, and the gleam

Of starlight, and the glowlight on the grass.

To secret things my hands committed him,

And strangely he hath thriven since that hour,

Ev'n as a leaf is fashion'd, ev'n as the hair

Of the long grass is woven, wondrously!

And thus, his brow bright with the balms of Earth,

He stands complete, his Father's child, my son.

O look upon him ! See his happy eyes !

And tell me that ye love him, and in turn

Will bless him, shielding him upon your breasts

If ever evil hour to him should come.

Oh, that sad rune we fear'd of old is false !

For gentle is he as the gentle things

Which foster'd him, too blest and beautiful

To be a terror or a grief to gods."

She ceased ; and Gefion thro' her loosen'd hair

Smiled, and stern Rota's look grew tenderer.

Then, stretch'd her listless length upon the grass,

Her dark face glowing brightly in the sun,

Upon one elbow leaning, sun-tanned Eir

Raised with quick wicked laugh her root and knife,

Saying, "O Frea, had I found him there

Fall'n like a flower in the dark arms of Earth,

This knife had made an end ; but since he stands

Full-grown and fair, immortal, and thy son,

I bid him welcome ! "—As she spake, the eyes

Of Balder fell upon the root and knife,

And lo, the knife gleam'd as a brand of gold,

While the black root, moist with the dews of earth,

Trembled, and blossom'd into light green leaves!

Then trembling, Eir arose, and stood her height,

While gazing full into her troubled eyes,

Bright Balder moved to embrace her silently.

But as he gently came there interposed

A wonder of new brightness,—such a shape,

So perfect in divine white loveliness,

As never mortal yet beheld and lived.

And Balder trembled, and his bosom heaved

With an exceeding sweetness strange and new,

While close to his there came a shining face,

Still as a sunbeam, dimmer than a dream.

And Freya, for 'twas she whose touch is life

To happy lovers and to loveless men

Is sickness and despair, said, breathing warm,

While on her alabaster arms love's light

Was flushing faint as thro' a rose's leaves,

" Let all my sisters greet thee as they will,

I *love* thee, Balder ! since of lovely things

Thou art the brightest and the loveliest!"

And lo! ere he was ware of her intent,

Unto his cheek she prest a warm red mouth

Kings of great empires would have swoon'd to touch,

And poets heavenly-dower'd would have died

To dream of kissing.   Then thro' Balder ran

A new miraculous rapture such as feels

The dark Earth when the scented Summer leaps

Full-blossom'd as a bridegroom to her arms;

Such as musk-roses know when blown apart

By sunbeams in mid-June; and Balder's sense

Swoon'd, and he seem'd strewn o'er with fruit and

  flowers,

And on his lids were touches like warm rain,

And on his nostrils and his parted lips

Delicious balm and spicy odours fell,

And all his soul was like a young maid's frame

Bathed in the warmth of love's first virgin dream.

Then, as he trembled thro' and thro' his form

With the last flush of that celestial fire,

The goddesses around him flocking came,

All giving welcome.   Some into his eyes

Gazed in such awe as pallid virgins feel

For some mysterious splendour masculine

They seek yet fear and shrink from as they touch.

For Balder's loveliness in that bright place

Was as the soft sheen of the summer moon

Arising silvern in the cloudless west

Above the sunset seas of orange gold ;

And there was trouble in his human eyes

Most melancholy sweet,—trouble like tears,

Or starlight, or the tremor of the dew.

'II.

THE FRUIT OF LIFE.

THEY led him to a bank with moss inlaid,

Close to the tranquil mirror of the sea,

And thither came pale ocean handmaidens

Singing to lutes of amber and of pearl,

While "Love him, love him," cried the goddesses,

"O love him, love him, he is beautiful!"

But Frea lifted up her hand, and cried,

"Love is not all—swear against all things ill

To watch him and protect him;"—and they cried,

"We swear! we swear!" Then bending over him

With bright black eyeballs burning into his,

Pale Rota touched his forehead with her spear,

Crying, "Live on! No touch of time shall cause

One wrinkle on thy smooth unruffled brow!"

And Eir, low-laughing, held with tender teeth,

Not bruising the fair skin, his naked arm,

And murmur'd, "Strength and subtle force be thine,

Drunk from my breath into thy deepest veins."
And Gefion, with her large, sad, heavenly eyes
Upgazing in his face, and one white hand
Laid softly on his side, cried, " As a tree
Be fruitful ! Wheresoe'er thou wanderest,
Fruitage go with thee and a thousand flowers !"
But Freya kiss'd him calmly on the brow,
And whisper'd to him lower than the rest,
" O Balder ! my soul's gift is best of all—
They bring thee life, but I have given thee love."

And Balder sank into a dream.   Much joy
Made his sense drowsy, and with happy eyes
He saw that mist of light and loveliness
Enclose him, while he seem'd as one who swims
Among the shallows of an orient sea.
A voice like music woke him, and he saw
Standing before him in light azure robes
A shape that 'midst those others seem'd as dim
And unsubstantial as a summer shade.
Tall was she, and her wondrous sheen of hair

Rain'd downward like the silvern willow's leaves,

And on her mystic raiment blue as heaven

There glimmer'd dewy drops like shining stars.

Pale was she, with the pallor of wan waters

That wash for evermore the cold white feet

Of spectral polar moons; and when she spake,

'Twas low as sea-wash on the starlit sands

And strange and far-away as sounds in sleep.

"Balder!" she sigh'd; and like a man who hears,

Upstarting on his bed, some wondrous cry,

Balder upstarted wildly listening.

"Balder! O brother Balder, whose fair face,

Ere yet I gazed upon it shining here,

I knew thro' dark eternities of dream,

See what *I* give thee! see what gentle gift

Thy sister Ydun brings thee: more divine

Than life's sweet breath, or the fair flame of love."

So·saying, from her veilëd breast she drew

Mystical apples like to diamond seeds,

So small to seeming that a score might lie

In the pink hollow of an infant's hand.

Each shone complete and pure as mother-o'-pearl

Touch'd with prismatic gleams of wondrous light,

And unto each on the scarce visible stem

There clung two perfect little leaves of gold.

This secret fruit the gods and goddesses

For ever feed on, evermore renewed;

And in a garden desolate and dim

Wash'd by the wild green sea of human graves,

Pale Ydun plucks it, and none other may.

" Eat ! " Ydun murmur'd—" Balder, eat and live—

This fruit shall slay the lingering taint of Earth

Within thee, and preserve thee all divine."

Then Balder reaching out his open'd hand

Did take the fruit, and eating of the same,

Which melted on his tongue like flakes of snow,

He felt thro' all his limbs the rapturous thrill

Of some supreme and unfamiliar life.

So leaving all those luminous shapes behind,

He took the hand of Ydun, kissing her

As moonlight kisses dew ; and side by side
They wended down across the yellow sands,—
And many hours they wander'd whispering low
Close to the bright edge of that sleeping Sea.

III.

THE CITY OF THE GODS.

So Balder knew what mystical delights,
What slumberous idleness and peace supreme
Belong to the immortal goddesses;
And not a goddess in those golden walks
But loved the human light in Balder's face.
At last there came a day (if day might come
Where suns sank never in the crystal sea)
When mighty Frea said, "The time is nigh
To say farewell—much yet remains to do,
A weary path to follow, ere thy seat
Among immortal creatures is secure."
And Balder smiled, for of those shining groves
His soul was weary tho' he knew it not;—
Ev'n Freya's kiss was chiller on his cheek,
And Gefion's face seem'd less serenely fair,
And only Ydun still had power to soothe
His spirit with her weirdly-woven runes.

And Balder said, " O Mother, sweet it is
To dwell among the immortals in these bowers,
But to fare on is better, and I seem
Ev'n as a cloud whose feet may never rest,
But still must wander, and it knows not whither."

And so from that fair valley silently
They pass'd, and up the mountain sides, and down
Thro' other prospects less divinely fair.

And from the valley they had left the face
Of Balder slowly faded like a star,
Forgotten, dwindled from the drowsy dream
Of those great slumberous-lidded goddesses.
From that bright realm's serene eternity
All forms that are not present fade away
Like shadows stealing o'er a summer stream.
Yea even Freya did forget his eyes,
And gazed straight out at the unchanging sea
Smiling all calm as if he had not been ;
And only Ydun did remember him,
Writing his name upon the yellow sands
And weaving it all round with subtle runes.

6

. . . But far away beyond those secret realms,

Still northward, thro' the wastes where nothing lives,

The goddess guided Balder, till at last

Into their faces flash'd the polar fires ;

So that the streams were purpled and the heights

Took deeper crimson gleams, and overhead

The stars were quench'd in amethyst and gold.

Then Frea pointed with her hand, and cried,

" Behold the CITY OF THE GODS ! "

                         They stood

Upon the verge of a vast Sea of Ice,

So rough, so sown with berg and drift, it seem'd

An ocean frozen in the midst of storm

Before the surge could break, the waves could fall.

Still was it 'neath the gleaming lights of heaven,

Silent and awful, sleeping with no stir,

In one vast gleam of crimson bright as blood

Cast on it from afar.   For lo ! beyond,

Rose Asgard the great City of the Gods,

For ever burnt to ashes night by night

And dawn by dawn for evermore renew'd.

And mortals when they see from out their caves

The City crumbling with a thousand fires

Cry, " Lo, the Sunset !"—and when evermore

They mark it springing up miraculous

From its own ashes strewn beside the sea,

Cry, "Lo, the Sunrise !" There, within its walls

The great gods strive in thickening fumes of fight,

Gathering together bloody ghosts of men ;

And when the great towers tremble and the spires

Shoot earthward and the fiery ashes smoke,

The gods exult a little space, and wave

Their brands for all the vales of earth to see ;

But when the ashes blacken, and the moon

Shines on the City's embers, silently

They creep into their starry tents and sleep,—

Till like a rose unfolding leaf by leaf,

The immortal City rises !

                    And behold !

There, far across the silent frozen Deep,

They saw the glimmer of the topmost towers,

Fading and changing in the lurid light

Of their own terrible consuming flame;
And shadows to and fro amid the gleam
Pass'd, smiting shadows, and from out the heavens
There came a far-off sound as of a sea.

Still onward, walking now with wearier feet
The ice of that great Ocean, they pursued
Their solitary way, and as they went,
With shadows ever lengthening to the south,
The City sank consuming, till its towers
Just touch'd with gold the red horizon fringe;
And in the darkening ether over it
A star sprang like a spirit clad in mail,
And sat without a sound upon its throne,
Down-gazing; and the empty heavens and air
Were troubled still with melancholy light,
Wherein the opening lamps of night were swung
Pure golden, twinkling without beams.

                              At last,
When of that City little more remain'd
Than splendour from its ashes fading slow,

They reach'd one mighty gateway crumbling down

Ev'n as a cloud that clings upon a crag,

And passing in they found the golden streets

All chill and desolate and strewn with shade;

For no quick foot of any living thing,

Mortal or god, trod there; but all around

Grew silence, and the luminous eyes of stars.

Then Frea said, "Call now upon the Father!"

And Balder, standing bright and beautiful

Like to a marble column wrought with gold,

All kindled with the shadows of the fire,

Rose on the ashes of the City and cried,

"Father!" when glory grew about his brow,

And on his breast and arms the light was shed,

Staining their alabaster.   So he stood,

Tall-statured, luminous, supremely fair,

Watch'd by the closing eyes of all the world.

And suddenly, in answer to his cry,

A fierce aurora of pale faces flash'd

Out of the night of the extremest north.

And Frea cried aloud, "Almighty gods!
Behold your brother Balder! Father in Heaven,
Behold thy Son!"

        From out the north there came
A murmur, and across the skies there swept
A trouble as of wildly waving hands.

Then Frea cried to Balder, "Call again!"

And Balder, shining still most beautiful,
And stretching out his arms to the black north,
Cried "Father!"

        Suddenly the stars were quench'd,
And heavy as a curtain fell the night.

IV.

THE VOICE OF THE FATHER.

THEN Frea said, " O Balder, best beloved,
My heart fails, and my weary spirit swoons.
Fare on alone, and enter unafraid
The presence of the Father."

As she spake,
Her face he saw not, but he felt her hands
Clinging around him, while his own fair face,
Amid that sudden darkness, shone serene,
Fearless and gentle, and his beauteous limbs
Gleam'd with the lustre of celestial life.
"Mother," he answer'd, "why is all so dark?
And where is he thou namest, that mine eyes
May look upon him?"

From the blacken'd ground
Her voice sobbed answer, saying, " Even now
His shadow is upon us. Pass *thou* on,

Glide silent thro' the phantom groves of gods,

And stand in thine immortal loveliness,

With eyes divine on his, before the throne.

Here will I linger, praying close to the earth,

Till thou returnest."

Shining like a star,

Spake Balder, " All is dim, and I discern

No pathway and no bourne;" but with clear voice

Uplifted like a swan's that flies thro' storm,

He call'd, "Where art thou, Father?   It is I,

Balder thy Son !"

As when the great seas roar

Suck'd in thro' weedy rocks and under-caves

With surging sorrow drearily prolong'd

In hoarse and billowy breaths of solemn sound,

Ev'n so that darkness murmur'd and a voice

Came thund'rous out of heaven with no words.

And Frea cried, "Thou hearest!   Hark, he calls—

Follow that murmur out into the dark,

And it shall guide thee to the Father's feet."

Silently, softly smiling, with no fear,

Balder pass'd on ; and as one gropes his way

Oceanward guided by the ocean's voice,

He faded slowly forth into the night.

V.

BALDER'S RETURN.

THERE close to the earth she waited, crouching down

'Mid the cold ashes of the sunken City,

While closing round her like to prison walls

The deep impenetrable darkness grew.

And soon it shed a heavy, weary rain,

That clung upon her, chilling soul and sense,

Cold as a corpse's lips; and all the while,

As a bird listens from its folded wings,

She listen'd!

           But the only sound she heard

Was the low murmur of that weary rain,

Which spread wet fingers o'er the shuddering heavens,

And drearily drew down the rainy lids

Over the gentle eyes of all the stars.

Silent she lay and hearken'd, till her soul

Had lost all count of time and faded back
Into its own sad, dumb eternity. . . .

At last she stirred like one that wakes from sleep.
The rain had ceased, the darkness to the north
Had lifted, and her eyes beheld afar,
Beneath the glimmer of the northern night,
The brightness of the god's returning feet.

Slowly, like one whose heart is heavy ; slowly,
Like one that muses sadly as he moves ;
Slowly, with darkness brooding at his back,
Came Balder, and his coming far away
Was ev'n as moonlight when the moon is sad
On misty nights of March ; and when again
He pass'd across the ashes of the City,
And she who bare him could behold his face,
'Twas spectral white, and in his heavenly eyes
There dwelt a shadowy pain.   Ev'n as a man
Who passing thro' the barrows of the slain
Hath seen the corpses sit at dead of night
Gazing in silence from their own green graves ;

Or as a maiden who hath seen a wraith

And knoweth that her shroud is being woven,

Came Balder out of heaven : still divine,

And beautiful, but ah ! how sorrowful ;

Still bright, but with a light as sadly fair,

Compared to that first splendour of the dawn,

As moonshine is to sunshine ; on his brow

The shade of some new sorrow, in his eyes

The birth of some new pity ; as a god,

Yet ghost-like, with deep glamour in his gaze,

Slowly, with faltering footsteps, Balder came.

Then Frea rose in silence, very pale,

For on her soul beholding Balder's face

Some desolate anticipation fell,

And turn'd her eyes on his, stretching her hands

To hold him and to embrace him, keen to hear

His message ; but he spake not when her arms

Were wound about him and upon his brow

Her soft kiss fell ; vacant his sad eyes seem'd,

As if they gazed on something far away.

Then Frea sobbed in agony of heart,

"Son, hast thou seen thy brethren?" and again,

"Son, hast thou seen thy Father?"   Yet a space

His lips were silent, and his eyes were blank,

But when again and yet again her tongue

Had framed the same fond question, Balder said,

In a low voice and a weary, "I have seen

My brethren and my Father!"   Like a man

Smit thro' and thro' with sudden sense of cold,

He shiver'd.

Then the goddess, mad to see

The light of agony on that well-loved face,

Clung to him wailing, "Balder! my Son Balder!

Why is thy look so sick, thy soul so weary?

What hast thou done and seen? what sight of heaven

Hath made thee sad?"—and Balder answer'd low

"O Mother! I have dream'd another dream—

I have seen my brethren in a dream—have seen

My brethren and my Father; and it seems

From that strange trance I have not waken'd yet,

But that I still am darkling in my dream,

The breath of gods about me, and the eyes

Of gods upon me !   Patience—question not—
The light is coming, and my soul is waking—
My dream grows clear, and I shall soon remember
All that mine eyes have seen, mine ears have heard."

Then on that City's ashes side by side
Sat son and mother, two colossal shapes,
Silent, in shadow ; but the eyes of heaven
Were opening above, and to the south
They saw the white seas flash with glittering bergs
In fitful glimmers to the windy night.
And when a little space had pass'd away
The god spake softly, saying, " All is clear,
My sorrow and my dream ; and Mother, now
I know those things which seem'd so sad and dark.
Ah ! woe is me that I was ever born
To be a terror and a grief to gods !"

Then Frea cried, " O Balder, unto whom
Can all the promise of thy beauty bring
Terror or grief?   Nay, 'twas with looks serene
To win the heart of heaven, that its wrath

Might never turn against thee, and to mock

With glory of thy human gentleness

The prophecy of that ancestral rune,

I bade thee go up beauteous and alone

Before the darkness of the Father's face.

Yet thou returnest barren of such joy

As thou a god shouldst snatch from gods thy kin,

First in thy plenitude beholding them ;

And on thy brow is sadness, not such peace

As comes from consecration of a kiss

Given by a Father to a son beloved

In whom he is well pleased ! ''

                    Then once again

Like a man smitten to the bone with cold,

Bright Balder shiver'd, and his beautiful face

Grew gray as any mortal's fix'd in death ;

And suddenly he cried, "O come away !

Come back to those green woods where I was born

The ways of heaven are dreary, and the winds

Of heaven blow chilly, and I fain would find

A refuge and a home !''

But Frea moan'd,

Turning her fair face northward in quick wrath,

"Ay me thy dream—I read it, from mine own

Most bitterly awaking. Woe to them!

Woe to the Father and the gods thy kin!

Out of thy mansion have they cast thee forth,

Denying thee thy birthright and thy seat

Up yonder at thy heavenly Father's side!"

But Balder, in a feeble voice and low,

Said, "They denied me nought, those Shapes I saw

Strangely as in a sleep; nay, but meseem'd

They pointed at me with their spectral hands

And waved me back, some with their raiment hems

Hiding their faces; in their eyes I saw

Not love but protestation absolute;

And when I rose and named my Father's name,

It seem'd creation rock'd beneath my feet

And all the cloudy void above my head

Trembled; and when I named my name, a voice

Shriek'd 'Balder!' and the naked vaults of heaven

Prolong'd in desolation and despair

The echoes of the word till it became

As thunder ! Then meseem'd I saw a hand,

Gripping the fiery lightning suddenly,

Strike at my head as if to smite me down ;

But tho' my frame was wrapt about with fire,

I stood unscathed ; and as I paused I saw,

Confused as stormy shadows in the sea,

Thrones gleaming, faces fading, starry shapes

Coming and going darkly ; and each time

I call'd upon my Father, that great hand

Flash'd down the fierce darts of the crimson
    levin,

And from that darkness which I knew was he

A voice came, and a cry that seem'd a curse,

Until my soul was sicken'd and afraid.

Then, for my heart was heavy, yearning still

To look upon him and to feel at last

The welcome of his consecrating kiss,

I fell upon my knees, folded my hands

Together, and I blest him ;—when methought

The voice wail'd, and the cry that seem'd a curse

Re-echoed. Then came blackness more intense ;

And for a space my sense and sight seem'd lost,

And when I woke I stood beside thee here,
Holding thy hand and looking in thine eyes."

Then Frea wail'd, " 'Tis o'er! my hope is o'er!
Thy Father loves thee not, but casts thee forth—
Where wilt thou find a place to rest thy feet?"
But Balder answer'd, " Where the cushat builds
Her nest amid green leaves, and where wild roses
Hang lamps to light the dewy feet of dawn,
And where the starlight and the moonlight slumber,
Ev'n there, upon the balmy lap of Earth,
Shall I not sleep again?   O Mother, Mother!
Pray to my Father that his soul may learn
To love me in due season, while again
Earthward we fare; and Mother, bless thou me,
Me whom my heavenly Father blesseth not,
With ministering hands before we go!"

Then Frea cried, blessing and kissing Balder,
" Go *thou*,—the green Earth loves thee, and thy face

Is as a lamp to all the gentle things

Which mingled in thy making—Go *thou* down,

But I will journey upward till I find

The footstool of the Father.   Night and day

With prayers, with intercession of deep tears,

With ministering murmurs, I will plead,

Low-lying like a cloud around his feet,

Thy cause, and the green Earth's which foster'd thee :

That in a later season love may come

In answer, and the Father fear no more

To seat thee 'mong Immortals at nis side.

Go down, my child, my sunbeam, my best-born,

My Balder, who art still deem'd beautiful

Save only in the heavenly Father's sight !

And when all things have blest thee; when all forms

Have gladden'd in thy glory ; when all voices,

The mountains and the rivers and the seas,

The white clouds and the stars upon their thrones,

Have known thy face and syllabled thy name ;

Come back again under the arch of heaven,

Not as a suppliant but a conqueror,

And take thy throne !"

The darkness far away
Groan'd : and the great void answer'd ; overhead
Cluster'd the countless spheres of night, like eyes
Downgazing ; but beneath the goddess' feet
Shot up dim gleams of dawn.

Then bright as day
Grew Balder, while his face, composed to peace,
Turn'd earthward ; and he stretch'd out eager arms
To that belovëd land where he was born.
"Farewell !" he said, and softly kiss'd the mother ;
Then, while the goddess glided like a cloud
Up heavenward, down to the dim Earth he pass'd
Slowly, with luminous feet.

. . . And when he came
To that cold realm which belts the Frozen Sea,
Behind his back the trumpets of the light
Were faintly blown ; a sudden sheen was thrown
Behind him and around him, wondrously ;
Bright shone the lonely waste of plain and berg ;
And reaching that great cape of porphyry

Which points with shadowy finger at the pole,

He turn'd his shining face once more, and watch'd ;

While far away in the remotest north

Bright Asgard, mystic City of the Gods,

Was rising from its ashes till its spires

Burnt golden in the rose-red arch of heaven.

IV.

BALDER'S RETURN TO EARTH.

BALDER'S RETURN TO EARTH.

I.

"BALDER IS HERE."

O who cometh sweetly
  With singing of showers?—
The wild wind runs fleetly
  Before his soft tread,
The sward stirs asunder
  To radiance of flowers,
While o'er him and under
  A glory is spread—
A white cloud above him
  Moves on thro' the blue,
And all things that love him
  Are dim with its dew :
The lark is upspringing,
  The merle whistles clear,

There is sunlight and singing,
  For Balder is here!

He walks on the mountains,
  He treads on the snows ;
He loosens the fountains
    And quickens the wells ;
He is filling the chalice
  Of lily and rose,
He is down in the valleys
    And deep in the dells—
He smiles, and buds spring to him,
  The bright and the dark ;
He speaks, and birds sing to him,
  The finch and the lark,—
He is down by the river,
  He is up by the mere,
Woods gladden, leaves quiver,
  For Balder is here.

There is some divine trouble
  On earth and in air—

Trees tremble, brooks bubble,
 Ants loosen the sod ;
Warm footfalls awaken
 Whatever is fair ;
Sweet rain-dews are shaken
 To quicken each clod.
The wild rainbows o'er him
 Are melted and fade,
The grass runs before him
 Thro' meadow and glade ;
Green branches close round him,
 The leaves whisper near—
" He is ours—we have found him—
 Bright Balder is here ! "

The forest glows golden
 Where'er he is seen,
New flowers are unfolden,
 New voices arise ;
Flames flash at his passing
 From boughs that grow green,

Dark runlets gleam, glassing
   The stars of his eyes.
The Earth wears her brightest
   Wherever he goes,
The hawthorn its whitest,
   Its reddest the rose ;
The days now are sunny,
   The white storks appear,
And the bee gathers honey,
   For Balder is here.

He is here on the heather,
   And here by the brook,
And here where together
   The lilac boughs cling ;
He is coming and going
   With love in his look,
His white hand is sowing
   Warm seeds, and they spring !
He has touch'd with new silver
   The lips of the stream,

And the eyes of the culver
  Are bright from his beam,
He has lit the great lilies
  Like lamps on the mere;
All happy and still is,
  For Balder is here.

Still southward with sunlight
  He wanders away—
The true light, the one light,
  The new light, is he!
With music and singing
  The mountains are gay,
And the peace he is bringing
  Spreads over the sea.
All night, while stars twinkling
  Gleam down on the glade,
His white hands are sprinkling
  With harebells the shade;
And when day hath broken,
  All things that dwell near

Will know, by that token,
    That Balder is here.

In the dark deep dominions
    Of pine and of fir,
Where the dove with soft pinions
    Sits still on her nest,
He sees her, and by her
    The young doves astir,
And smiling sits nigh her,
    His hand on her breast;
The father-dove lingers
    With love in its eyes,
Alights on his fingers,
    And utters soft cries,
And the sweet colours seven
    Of the rainbow appear
On its neck, as in heaven,
    Now Balder is here.

He sits by a fountain
    Far up near the snow,

And high on the mountain
   The wild reindeer stand;
On crimson moss near to him
   They feed walking slow,
Or come with no fear to him,
   And eat from his hand.
He sees the ice turning
   To columns of gold,
He sees the clouds burning
   On crags that were cold;
The great snows are drifting
   To cataracts clear,
All shining and shifting,
   For Balder is here.

O who sitteth singing,
   Where sunset is red,·
And wild ducks are winging
   Against the dark gleam?
It is he, it is Balder,
   He hangeth his head

Where willow and alder
　　Droop over the stream ;
And the purple moths find him
　　And hover around,
And from marshes behind him
　　He hears a low sound :
The frogs croak their greeting
　　From swamp and from mere,
And their faint hearts are beating,
　　For Balder is here.

The round moon is peeping
　　Above the low hill ;
Her white light, upcreeping
　　Against the sun's glow,
On the black shallow river
　　Falls silvern and chill,
Where bulrushes quiver
　　And wan lilies grow.
The black bats are flitting,
　　Owls pass on soft wings,

Yet silently sitting
　　He lingers and sings—
He sings of the Maytime,
　　Its sunlight and cheer,
And the night like the daytime
　　Knows Balder is here.

He is here with the moonlight,
　　With night as with day,
The true light, the one light,
　　The new light, is he ;
The moon-bows above him
　　Are melted away,
And the things of night love him,
　　And hearken and see.
He sits and he ponders,
　　He walks and he broods,
Or singing he wanders
　　'Neath star-frosted woods ;
And the spheres from afar, light
　　His face shining clear :

8

Yea, the moonlight and starlight
  Feel Balder is here.

He is here, he is moving
  On mountain and dale,
And all things grow loving,
    And all things grow bright:
Buds bloom in the meadows,
  Milk foams in the pail,
There is scent in the shadows,
    And sound in the light:
O listen! he passes
  Thro' valleys of flowers,
With springing of grasses
  And singing of showers.
Earth wakes—he has called her,
  Whose voice she holds dear;
She was waiting for Balder,
    And Balder is here!

II.

'MID mountains white by rainbows spanned,
   Upon his knees he sank,
And melted in his hollow'd hand
   The stainless snows, and drank.

And far beneath in mists of heat
   Great purple valleys slept,
And flashing bright beneath his feet
   The loosen'd cataracts leapt.

Down to those happy vales he drew
   Where men and women dwell,
And white snow melted, green grass grew,
   Where'er his footprints fell.

Then night by night and day by day
   His deepest joy was found

In watching happy things of clay
　And hearing human sound.

All human eyes to him were sweet,
　He loved the touch of hands,
He kissed the print of human feet
　Upon the soft sea-sands.

Most silently he went and came,
　With mild and blissful mien,
Bright as a beam his face would flame
　Amid the forests green.

To timid mortals passing by
　He seemed a vision fair,
But little children oft drew nigh,
　And let him smooth their hair ;

And witless men would come to him
　With wild and eldritch cries,
And lying in the moonbeams dim
　Would gaze into his eyes !

His voice was in the lonely wood,
  And by the nameless stream,—
He shed in silent solitude
  The peaceful rays of dream.

From vale to vale he went, and blest
  The wild beast and the bird,—
While deep within the glad Earth's breast
  The founts of being stirred. . . .

He sat down in a lonely land
  Of mountain, moor, and mere,
And watch'd, with chin upon his hand,
  Dark maids that milk'd the deer.

And while the sun set in the skies,
  And stars shone in the blue,
They sang sweet songs, till Balder's eyes
  Were sad with kindred dew.

He passed along the hamlets dim
  With twilight's breath of balm,

And whatsoe'er was touch'd by him
Grew beautiful and calm.

The old man sitting on the grass
Look'd up 'neath hoary hair,
And felt some heavenly presence pass
And gladden'd unaware!

He came unto a hut forlorn
As evening shadows fell,
And saw the man among the corn,
The woman at the well.

And entering the darken'd place,
He found the cradled child;
Stooping he lookt into its face,
Until it woke and smiled!

Then Balder passed into the night
With soft and shining tread,
The cataract called upon the height,
The stars gleam'd overhead.

He raised his eyes to those cold skies
   Which he had left behind,—
And saw the banners of the gods
   Blown black upon the wind.

He watch'd them as they came and fled,
   Then his divine eyes fell.
"I love the green Earth best," he said,
   "And I on Earth will dwell!"

III.

ALL THINGS BLEST BY BALDER.

So when his happy feet had wander'd far,

When all the birds had brighten'd and his hand

Had linger'd on the brows of all the beasts,

He came among the valleys where abode

Mortals that walk erect upon the ground.

First, southward passing, he beheld those men

Who, where the snow for ever lieth, dwell

In caverns of the ground and swathe their limbs

In skins of beasts : these felt his glory pass,

But knew it not, because their eyes were dim

With many nights of darkness.   Round their doors

Sorrel blood-red he cast and saxifrage,

And singing passed away !   Then roam'd he on,

Past porphyry and greenstone crags that line

Limitless oceans of unmelting ice,

Until he enter'd valleys kindlier

That redden'd into ruby as he came ;
And in among the countless deer he stole,
Marking their horns with golden moss, and singing
A strange soft song their souls could understand.

Then as the Earth grew fairer, presently
He came beneath the shade of forest leaves,—
And deep among the emerald depths he found
Those mortal men who dwell in woods and build
Their dwellings of the scented boughs of trees.
And often, with his cheek upon his hand,
Balder would sit and watch the smoke of fire
Upcurling thro' the branches heavenward,
While to and fro in sunshine passed the shapes
Of men and women.   Most he loved to mark
Those forms which gods made fairest, and to hear
Those voices gods made sweetest ; but his hand,
Falling unseen, was gentlest on the hair
Of children and of hoary aged men.

Then Balder said, " The Earth is fair, and fair,
Yea fairer than the stormy lives of gods,

The lives of gentle dwellers on the Earth ;
For shapen are they in the likenesses
Of goddesses and gods, and on their limbs
Sunlight and moonlight mingle, and they lie
Happy and calm in one another's arms
O'er-canopied with greenness ; and their hands
Have fashion'd fire that springeth beautiful
Straight as a silvern lily from the ground,
Wondrously blowing ; and they measure out
Glad seasons by the pulses of the stars.
O Spirit whom I know not, tho' I fear
Thy shadow on my soul where'er I go,
Almighty Father, tho' thou lov'st me not,
I love thy children !   I could sit all hours,
Just looking into their still heavenly eyes,
Holding their hands !   Most dear they are to me,
Because they are my brethren ;—beautiful,
My brethren and thy children !"

                    O'er his head
The blue sky darken'd, and a thund'rous voice
Murmur'd afar off,—and in great black drops

Came out of heaven the blind and desolate rain.

But Balder gazing upward reach'd out arms

And bless'd it as it fell; and lo, it grew

Silvern and lovely as an old man's hair!

And scents came out of the rich-soilèd earth,

And all the boughs were glad and jewel-hung,

Till very softly, very silently,

The shower ceased, with kisses tremulous

On Balder's lifted hands!

            Even so he turn'd

The saddest things to beauty.   With his face

Came calm and consecration; and the Earth

Uplifting sightless eyes in a new joy,

Answer'd the steadfast smile of the still heavens

With one long look of peace.   In those strange days

The wild wind was his playmate,—yea, the blast

New-loosen'd by the very hands of gods

Leapt to him like a lamb, and at his smile

Fell at his feet, and slept.   Then out of heaven

Came lightnings, from whose terror every face

Of humankind was hidden,—meteors, flames,

Forms of the fiery levin, such as wait

For ever at the angry beck of gods.

But Balder stood upon a promontory,

And saw them shining o'er the open sea,

And on the fields of ether crimson'd red ;

And lo, he lifted up a voice and cried,

" O beautiful wild children of the fire,

Whence come ye, whither go ye?   Be at peace,

Come hither ! " and like soft white stingless snakes

That crawl on grass, the fiery meteors came,

Licking his feet in silence, looking up

With luminous eyes !

        Ev'n as he conquer'd these,

Heaven's fiery messengers, he tamed the hearts

Of human things, and in the sun they sat

Weaving green boughs, or wooing in the shade,

Or leading home the white and virgin bride.

For as the holy hunger and desire

Came quickening in the hearts of birds and beasts,

Ev'n so woke love within the hearts of men ;

And out of love came children ; and the Earth

Was merry with new creatures thronging forth

Like ants that quicken on the sun-kist sod.

IV.

THE CRY FROM THE GROUND.

AND Balder bends above them, glory-crown'd,
Marking them as they creep upon the ground,
Busy as ants that toil without a sound,
   With only gods to mark.

But list ! O list ! what is that cry of pain,
Faint as the far-off murmur of the main ?
Stoop low and hearken, Balder !   List again !
   " Lo ! Death makes all things dark !"

Ay me, it is the earthborn souls that sigh,
Coming and going underneath the sky ;
They move, they gather, clearer grows their cry—
   O Balder, bend, and hark !

The skies are still and calm, the seas asleep,
In happy light the mortal millions creep,

Yet listen, Balder!—still they murmur deep,

"Lo! Death makes all things dark."

[Oh, listen! listen!] "Blessed is the light,

We love the golden day, the silvern night,

The cataracts leap, the woods and streams are bright,

We gladden as we mark.

"Crying we come, but soon our cheeks are dried—

We wander for a season happy-eyed,

And we forget how our gray sires have sigh'd,

'Lo! Death makes all things dark.'

"For is the sun not merry and full of cheer?

Is it not sweet to live and feel no fear?

To see the young lambs leaping, and to hear

The cuckoo and the lark?

"Is toil not blest, is it not blest to be?

To climb the snows, to sail the surging sea,

To build our saeters where our flocks roam free?

But Death makes all things dark.

" Is love not blest, is it not brave and gay
With strong right hand to bear one's bride away,
To woo her in the night time and the day
  With no strange eyes to mark?

And blest are children, springing fair of face
Like gentle blossoms in the dwelling-place ;
We clasp them close, forgetting for a space
  Death makes the world so dark.

" And yet though life is glad and love divine,
This Shape we fear is here i' the summer shine,—
He blights the fruit we pluck, the wreath we twine,
  And soon he leaves us stark.

" He hunts us fleetly on the snowy steep,
He finds us as we sow and as we reap,
He creepeth in to slay us as we sleep,—
  Ah! Death makes all things dark !

"Yea, when afar over our nets hang we,
He walks unto us even on the sea ;

The wind blows in his hair, the foam flies free

    O'er many a sinking bark !

" Pity us, gods, and take this god away,

Pity us, gods, who made us out of clay,

Pity us, gods, that our sad souls may say,

    ' Bright is the world, which Death a space made

      dark.' "

V.

THE SHADOW ON THE EARTH.

Now all his peace was poison'd and he found
No solace in the shining eyes of day,
Starlight and moonlight now seem'd sorrowful,
And in his soul there grew the sense of tears.
For wheresoe'er he wander'd, whatsoe'er
He gazed on, whether in the light or dark,
Was troubled by a portent.

                     Evermore,
Listening to nature's sad unceasing moan,
Balder remember'd that pale haunting Shape
Which he had seen in those primæval woods
Where he was foster'd by the happy Earth ;
And those sad tales the mother-goddess told
Of mortal men, and how they waste and wane,
Came back upon his life with fearful gleams.

Yea, Balder's heart was heavy.   All in vain

He wove wild runes around the flowers and trees,

And round the necks of beasts and gentle birds;

For evermore the cold hand found them out,

And evermore they darkly droop'd and died.

This direful thing was on the helpless Earth,

Unprison'd, unconfined.   Before his face

It faded, and before his eager touch

Melted and changed, but evermore again

It gather'd into dreadful lineaments,

And passed with arms outreaching on its way.

Then Balder lifted up his trembling hands

To heaven, crying, "FATHER!" and no sound

Came from the frozen void; and once again,

"O Mother, Mother!" but pale Frea lay

Stone-still in anguish at the Father's feet,

And dared not answer; and he cried once more,

"Gods, gods, immortal gods!" when suddenly

He saw across the open arctic heaven

The hosts of Asgard, ev'n as sunset clouds

That drift confusedly in masses bright,

Trooping, with blood-red rays upon their heads,

To fight against the meteor snakes that flash

Far northward in the white untrodden wastes.

They passed, they saw not, but he heard their feet

Afar as muffled thunder, and he cried,

" O Slayers of the snake, immortal gods,

Come hither and slay the slayer, that the world

May rest in peace ! "

      If ever his faint cry

Reach'd to their ears, the dark gods only smiled,

With smiles like sullen lightning on the lips

Of tempest ; and he found no comfort there.

Nor from the mouths of flower, or bird, or tree,

Sea-fern, or sighing shell upon the shore,

Came any answer when he question'd low,

" What is this thing ye fear ? who sent it hither,

This shape which moaning mortals christen Death ? "

But from the darkness of his own heart's pity,

And from all things in unison—the gloom

Of midnight, and the trouble of the clouds,

From sunless waters, solitary woods,

There came a murmur, " None can answer thee,

Save him thou followest with weary feet ! "

Wherefore he wander'd on, and still in vain

Sought Death the slayer.   Into burial-places,

Heapen with stones and seal'd with slime of grass,

He track'd him, found him sitting lonely there

Like one that dreams, his dreadful pitiless eyes

Fix'd on the sunset star.   Or oftentimes

Beheld him running swiftly like a wolf

Who scents some stricken prey along the ground.

Or saw him into empty huts crawl slow,

And while the man and woman toiled i' the field,

Gaze down with stony orbs a little space

Upon the sickly babe, which open'd eyes,

And laugh'd, and spread its little faded hands

In elfin play. Nay, oft in Balder's sight

The form seem'd gentle, and the fatal face

Grew beautiful and very strangely fair.

Yet evermore while his swift feet pursued,

Darkling it fled away, and evermore

Most pitiful rose cries of beasts and birds,

Most desolate rose moans of stricken men,
Till Balder wept for sorrow's sake, and cried,
" Help me, my Father ! "

                   Even as he spake,
A gray cloud wept upon the Earth, which wore
A gentle darkness ; and the wastes and woods,
The mountains trembling in their hoary hair,
The mighty continents and streams and seas,
Uplifted a low voice of mystery
And protestation. Then a wingèd wind
Caught up the sound and bore it suddenly
To the great gates of Asgard, so that all
Within the shadowy City heard ; and He
Who sitteth far beyond upon his throne,
Immortal, terrible, and desolate,
Heard, but was silent ; and no answer came,
No help or answer, from the lips of heaven.

VI.

ON THE HEIGHTS—EVENING.

MOUNTAIN GIRL.

ART thou a god? thy brow is shining so!
O thou art beautiful!   What is thy name?

BALDER.

Balder.

GIRL.

Now let me look into thy face.

BALDER.

Look.

GIRL.

How I love thee!

BALDER.

And *thy* name?

GIRL.

Snow-blossom.

That is my mother standing at the door,
Shading her face and gazing up the hill.
I keep my mother's reindeer, and each night
Milk them, and drive them to their pasturage.
How clear thine eyes are ! They are like that star
Up yonder, twinkling on the snow !

BALDER.

Come hither !

Thou hast bright hair like mine, and starry eyes,
Snow-blossom, and a voice like falling water ;
Thy flesh is like the red snow and the white
Mingled together softly, and thy breath
Is scented like the fragrant thyme in flower.
Mine eyes have look'd on many shapes like thine—
Yet thou art fairest.

GIRL.

I am call'd Snow-blossom

Because I am not brown like other maids,
And when a little child I was so white !

BALDER.

Snow-lily !

GIRL.

They are calling—I must go—
Come down with me, and by our saeter's fire
Slumber this night, and ere thou liest down
I'll sing to thee the strange old songs I know
Of Death, and of the battle-fields of gods,
And of the wondrous City where they dwell
Yonder afar away !

BALDER.

What knowest *thou*

Of Death or gods ?

GIRL.

Only last winter tide
I saw my father die : he drew one breath,
Then went to sleep ; but when we touch'd his hands

They had no warmth, and his twain eyes were glazed,

Gazing at something that we saw not.   Then

We wrapt him warm in skins and in his hands

We set his seal-spear and his seal-hide thong,

And placed him sitting in the sunless earth,

Crouch'd resting on the ground with knees drawn up

As many a night he sat beside the fire.

And that the fierce white bear might find him not,

We wall'd him up with earth and mighty stones,

Seal'd tight with snow and water : then we said

A prayer to the good gods, and left him there

Where they might find him.

BALDER.

Hast thou seen that Death

Which smote thy father?

GIRL.

Nay!—no mortal thing

Sees him and lives.   He walks about the Earth

At his good will, and smites whate'er he lists,

Both young and old.   There is no spirit at all
More strong than he !

BALDER.

Is he a god?

GIRL.

I know not.

BALDER.

And will thy father waken ?

GIRL.

When the gods
Find out his grave, and open up the stones,
Then he will waken, and will join the hosts
Of Hermod and of Thor ; for he was brave,
My father : he could keep his own, and ere
He took my mother, with his spear he slew
Her father and her brother, who were wroth
Because they hated him ; and evermore
When he shed blood, he made his offering
To Hermod and the rest.

BALDER.

And thou, Snow-blossom,
Thou in thy turn wilt wed a mighty man,
And bear strong children?

GIRL.

Yes!—a man of strength,
Fair like my father.   I would have him fierce
As bears are, bearded, a seal-strangler, swift,
And a great hunter with a boat and dogs.
But I would have him very cunning too,
Knowing old songs and wise at weaving runes,
That in the season when the sun is fled
We might be merry thro' the long cold nights
Waiting for summer!

BALDER.

Hark!

GIRL.

It is my mother
Calling again!   Wilt thou not come?

BALDER.

Go thou !

I shall fare further o'er the summer hills.

Snow-blossom !   Let me kiss thee ere thou goest !

GIRL.

Yes !

BALDER.

Now farewell ! . . .

How lightly down the height

She leapeth with the leaping cataract,

And now she turns and waves her little hand,

And plunging down she fades.   And in the world

Dwell countless thousands beautiful as she,

Happy and virgin, drinking with no pain

The vital air of heaven !   O pink flesh

Over the warm nest of a singing heart

Heap'd soft as blossoms !   O strange starry eyes

Of mortals, beautiful as mine !   O flame

Out of soft nostrils trembling, like the light

From lips of flowers !   O wonder of Earth's life,

Why is it that the great gods chase thee down?
Why is it that thou fallest evermore
When thou art fairest?   Up and down the world
Each creature walks, and o'er each red mouth hangs
Breath like a little cloud, faint smoke of breath
Blown from the burning of the fire within.
Great gods, if as they say ye fashion'd them,
Why do ye suffer this wild wind of doom
To wither what ye made so wonderful?

The vale is dark, the snow-fields on the height
Are purpled with the midnight. . . . . Steadfastly
One lamp shines in the valley, and above
The still star shines an answer.   Slumber well,
Snow-blossom!   May no shadow of the gods
Come near to trouble thee in thy repose!
Sleep like immortal raiment wrap thee round,
To charm away the rayless eyes of Death!

VII.

THE VOW OF BALDER.

BRIGHT Balder cried, " Curst be this thing
  Which will not let man rest,
Slaying with swift and cruel sting
  The very babe at breast !

" On man and beast, on flower and bird,
  He creepeth evermore ;
Unseen he haunts the Earth ; unheard
  He crawls from door to door.

" I will not pause in any land,
  Nor sleep beneath the skies,
Till I have held him by the hand
  And gazed into his eyes ! "

BALDER'S QUEST FOR DEATH.

I.

HE sought him on the mountains bleak and bare
　　And on the windy moors ;
He found his secret footprints everywhere,
　　Yea ev'n by human doors.

All round the deerfold on the shrouded height
　　The starlight glimmer'd clear ;
Therein sat Death, wrapt round with vapours white
　　Touching the dove-eyed deer.

And thither Balder silent-footed flew,
　　But found the phantom not ;
The rain-wash'd moon had risen cold and blue
　　Above that lonely spot.

Then as he stood and listen'd, gazing round
  In the pale silvern glow,
He heard a wailing and a weeping sound
  From the wild huts below.

He mark'd the sudden flashing of the lights,
  He heard cry answering cry—
And lo! he saw upon the silent heights
  A shadowy form pass by.

Wan was the face, the eyeballs pale and wild,
  The robes like rain wind-blown,
And as it fled it clasp'd a naked child
  Unto its cold breast-bone.

And Balder clutch'd its robe with fingers weak
  To stay it as it flew—
A breath of ice blew chill upon his cheek,
  Blinding his eyes of blue.

'Twas Death! 'twas gone!—All night the shepherds
    sped,
    Searching the hills in fear;

At dawn they found their lost one lying dead
    Up by the lone black mere ;

And lo ! they saw the fatal finger-mark,
    Which reacheth young and old,
Seal'd, livid still, upon its eyelids dark
    And round its nipples cold.

Then Balder moan'd aloud and smote his breast,
    " O drinker of sweet breath,
Curst be thy cruel lips ! I shall not rest
    Until I clasp thee, Death ! "

He track'd the footprints in the morning gray
    From rocky haunt to haunt.
Far up the heights a wolf had crost Death's way ;
    It lay there, lean and gaunt.

He reach'd the highest snows and found them strewn
    With bleaching bones of deer. . . .
Night came again,—he listen'd 'neath the moon
    Shining most cold and clear.

Beneath him stretch'd vast valleys green and fair,
    Still in the twilight shine,
With great waste tarns and cataracts hung in air,
    And woods of fir and pine ;

And on the tarns lay dim red dreams of day
    The midnight sun cast there,—
Sunlight and moonlight blending in one ray
    Of mother-o'-pearl most fair.

He wander'd down thro' woods that fringed the snows,
    Down cliffs with ivy crown'd,
He passed by lonely tarns whence duskly rose
    Great cranes, and hover'd round.

He paused upon a crimson crag, and lo !
    Deep down at the crag's foot,
The Shape he sought, in shadow, far below,
    With folded wings, sat mute !

Ev'n as a vulture of the east it seem'd
    Brooding on something dead ;

Dark was the form on which its cold eyes gleam'd,
    And still and heavy as lead.

Then Balder swung himself from tree to tree,
    And reach'd the fatal place ! . . .
The phantom fled as silent wild things flee,
    But a white human face

Gleam'd from the ground ; and Balder's glory shone
    On a wild cowherd's hair !
Too late—his cheeks were chill—his breath was gone—
    His bosom torn and bare.

The Shape unseen had cast him o'er the steep,
    Down, down, the abysses dim,—
Then, as an eagle followeth a sheep,
    Had flutter'd after him !

His bearskin dress was bloody ; in his grip
    He clutch'd a cowherd's horn ;
His eyes were glazed, and on his stainèd lip
    Death's kisses lay forlorn.

But Balder touch'd him and his face grew fair,
    Shining beneath the skies,
Yea, Balder crost his hands, and smooth'd his hair,
    And closed his piteous eyes. . . .

Not resting yet, the bright god wander'd soon
    Down by the torrent's track ;
And lo ! a sudden glory hid the moon,
    And dawn rose at his back.

II.

Dawn purple on the peaks, and pouring in floods
    Into the valleys fair,
Encrimsoning the lakes and streams and woods,
    Illuming heaven and air.

And every creature gladden'd, and the Earth
    Turn'd on her side and woke :
There came sweet music ; sunny gleams of mirth
    Across the landscape broke.

And when a thousand eyes of happy things
    Had open'd all around,
And when each form that blooms, each form that
    sings,
    Saw Balder glory-crown'd,

Standing like marble bathed in liquid flame,
    Perfect of face and limb,

Infinite voices syllabled his name,
    And Earth smiled up at him !

All shapes that knew him (and all shapes that be
    Knew Balder's face that hour)
Grew glorified—the torrent and the tree,
    The white cloud and the flower.

The meres flash'd golden mirrors for his face ;
    The forests saw and heard ;
The cataracts brighten'd ; in its secret place
    The sunless runlet stirred.

A light of green grass ran before his feet,
    His brow was bright with dew,
Where'er he trod there sprang a flower full sweet,
    Rose, crimson, yellow, or blue.

But Balder's face was pale, altho' his frame
    Its natal splendour wore ;
Altho' the green Earth gladden'd as he came,
    God Balder's soul was sore.

"O happy Earth! O happy beams of day!
  O gentle things of breath!
Blest were ye, if some hand divine might slay
  The slayer, even Death!"

He spake, and he was answer'd. By his side
  A crimson river ran,
Out of the cloven mountains spreading wide
  It water'd vales for man.

Amid its shallows flowers and sedge did twine,
  But in the midst 'twas deep,
And on its sides fed flocks of goats and kine
  O'er meadows soft as sleep.

Suddenly, while upon its marge he stood,
  His heart grew cold as clay,—
For lo! the phantom! sailing down the flood,
  Dim in the dawn of day! . . .

'Mid drifted foxglove-bells and leaves of green
  Uptorn and floating light,

There came, with face upturn'd, now hid, now seen,
　　A maiden dark as night—

Her raven hair was loosen'd, her soft breath
　　Had fled and left no stir,
Her eyes were open, looking up at Death,
　　Who drifted down with her.

Beside her, tangled 'mid the foxglove-bells,
　　A shepherd's crook was cast,
While softly on the water's silvern swells
　　Her form was floating past.

And lo! with eyes of feverish fatal light
　　Fix'd on her face in dream,
Death clung unto her 'mid the eddies bright
　　Upon the shining stream.

And Balder wail'd; and wafted down that way,
　　Death saw his shape and knew,—
Then, like a falcon startled from its prey,
　　Rose, vanishing from view!

III.

THE FIGHT OF SHIPS.

Now Balder came across the great sea-shore,

And saw far out upon the windless waves

A fight of water-dragons fierce as fire,

Wingèd and wild and wrought about with gold.

And dragon unto dragon clash'd and clung,

And each shriek'd loud, and teeth in teeth were set,

Until the sea was crimson'd, and one sank

In its own blood. So like to living things

They seem'd, but ships they were within whose
    wombs

Throbbed many savage hearts. And suddenly,

Amid that clangour of sharp steel and shriek

Of living voices, 'mid the thick o' the fight,

When in the stainèd waters all around

Men to the brain were cloven as they swam,

Balder saw dimly, hovering on wings,

Ev'n as the kestrel hovers poised and still

With glittering eyes searching the nether ground,

The Shape he sought.   As the bright dragons rush'd

This way and that with rapid sweep of oars,

And as the tumult passed from wave to wave,

It follow'd, as the falcon followeth

Some fearful quarry creeping on the ground.

And when the sunset came, and the great din

Was hush'd, and torn apart from one another

The dragons darken'd on a fiery sea,

The Shape, illumined with a crimson gleam,

Still linger'd o'er them very quietly,

Scenting the slain that drifted like to weeds

On the red waters, shoreward.

                         Then aloud

Cried Balder, "FATHER!" uttering from his heart

A bitter moan, and as he spake he saw,

All congregating on the brazen walls

Of sunset, with their wild eyes looking down,

Feeding upon the carnage of the fight,

The gods his kin ; and like to evening clouds,

Crimson and golden in the sunset flame,

They would perchance have seem'd to human eyes,

But his perceived them clearly and discern'd

The rapture in their faces as they gazed.

Yet ne'ertheless he cried, "Come down, ye gods,

And help me, that upon this fatal thing

I lay my hand!" They laugh'd reply, and lo!

He saw their banners raised i' the wind, their brands

Flashing and moving.

"FATHER!"

No reply;

But quiet as a curtain fell the night,

Solemn, without a star.

Then by the sea

Silent walk'd Balder, and all sounds were still

Beyond him on the bosom of the deep.

And where he went along the moonless sands

He made a brightness such as ocean shells

Keep in their iris'd ears; and the soft sea

Came singing round his silvern feet; and doves

Came out of caves and lit upon his hands.

Then Balder thought, "He answer'd, and has sent

The darkness as a token!" and ev'n then

He *blest* his father.

. . . . What is this that flames,

Lurid and awful, out upon the sea?

What dusky radiance, tho' the world is dark,

Shoots like a comet yonder upon the sky?

Seized in the fangs of fire, a dragon-ship

Consumes and shrieks, and as it burns illumes

The water under and the thunderous rack

Blackening above; and Balder as he stands

Pallid upon a headland, on his face

Catches the red reflection of the ray;

Ocean and sky are crimson'd, and he sees

Black shapes that hither and thither, waving arms,

Dart 'midst the flame on the consuming decks

And plunge with shrill scream down into the sea.

What care to call on the Immortals now?

He looks, one hand prest hard in agony

Upon his aching heart, and he discerns,

Brooding above that brightness, poised i' the air,

Down gazing, half illumed, half lost in light,

The Phantom !   As the ship consumes and fades,

And as the last cry rises on the air,

The Shape sinks lower with no waft of wing.

And when in dumb and passionate despair,

Balder looks northward once again, he sees

The cloud-rack parted, the cold north on fire,

And all the gods, with cruel cheeks aflame

And bright eyes glittering like cluster'd stars,

Thronging against the blacken'd bars of Heaven.

IV.

YDUN.

THEN Balder lifted up his voice and cried,

" Curst be this thing and you who sent it hither,

Tho' ye be gods, immortal, and my kin ;

For now I loathe you, deeming lovelier far

The black hawk, and the fox upon the ground,

Who slay sweet lives not knowing what they do ;

But ye, O gods, are wise, yet Death's sick scent

Is pleasant to your nostrils."   Loudly afar

A laugh of thunder answer'd, and the shapes

Still congregated in the glistening north

Flash'd like the pale aurora one white gleam

Of earthward-looking eyes, and in the midst

A hoary Face like to a moonlit cloud,

Silent, and staring down with orbs of stone.

And on this last did Balder gaze, and lo !

He shiver'd cold, his cheek divine was blanch'd,

And with no further word he turn'd away.

. . . So walk'd he by the Ocean, till that gleam

Far outupon the crimson waters died ;

Till night grew deeper and all sounds were still'd.

And all that night his human heart was turn'd

Against the gods his kin, against the god

His father ; for he thought, "He made this thing,

He sent it hither to the happy Earth ;

And when it slays they gladden in the halls

Of Asgard, and no pity fills their hearts

For gentle stricken men."   Long hours he paced

The cold sands of the still black sea ; and where

His foot fell moonlight lay and live sea-snails

Crept glimmering with pink horns ; and close to shore

He saw the legions of the herring flash,

Swift, phosphorescent, on the surface shining

Like bright sheet-lightning as they came and went.

At intervals, from the abyss beyond,

Came the deep roar of whales.

                              Betimes he stood

Silent, alone, upon a promontory

And now about him like white rain there fell
The splendour of the moonlight. All around
The calm sea rolled upon the rocks or drew
Dark surges from the caverns, issuing thence
Troubled and churn'd to boiling pools of foam.
Erect he stood, uplifting his white hands;
For round him on the slippery weed-hung reefs,
Outcreeping from the blackness of the sea,
In legions came the flocks of gentle seals
And gray sea lions with their lionesses.
And o'er the rocks they clomb till all the place
Was blacken'd, and the rest upon the sea,
Their liquid eyeballs in the moonlight burning,
Swam round and round with necks outstretch'd to gaze;
And those beneath him touch'd his shining feet,
And when he raised his hand and blest them all,
Uplifted heads like happy flocks of sheep
Bleating their joy!

   Ev'n then he heard a voice
Cry "Balder!" thrice, and turning he beheld
Standing above him on the promontory

A spirit he remember'd; for her hair
Swept downward like the silvern willow's leaves,
And on her mystic raiment blue as heaven
There glimmer'd dewy drops like heavenly stars.
And as he turn'd unto her he perceived
Her deathlike pallor, and he straightway knew
He look'd on Ydun, who had given to him
Those mystic apples which immortal forms
For ever feed on evermore renew'd.

And Ydun said, " O Balder, I could hear
Thy lone cry yonder in the silent realms
Where, gathering golden asphodels in meads
Of starlight under the dark Tree, I stray'd;
And all my heart was troubled for thy sake,
My brother, and I came across the worlds
To seek thee, bringing in my veilèd breast
More fruits to heal thee and to make thee strong
Despite the gods who love thee not, thy kin;
For I who bring them love thee, knowing well
There stands no shape in the celestial halls
So beautiful as thou ! "

And as she spake
She drew the apples forth and proffer'd them
To Balder's lips; but on those lips there lay
An ashen tinge as of mortality.
And taking not the gift he answer'd low,
" O Ydun, let me give thy gift to men,
That *they* may eat and live ! "

'But Ydun said,
While on his cheek he felt her breath come cold
As frosty moonlight,—" Name them not, but eat—
Eat *thou*, and live.   O Balder, men were born
To gather earthly fruit a little space,
And then, grown old with sudden lapse of years,
To wither up and die ; and fruit like this
Could never light on any human lip
The flame-like breath of immortality.
Flesh are they, and must fall ; spirits are we,
And fed with life diviner, we endure."

Then Balder said, " Dost thou not weep for them ?
Poor mortals with their shadows on the ground,

Yet kin to thee and me ! He made them fair

As we are, tho' they sicken and are slain ;

Yea, by a god accurst that haunts the world

Their hearts are set asunder, and their teeth

Devour each other. Lo ! the beautiful Earth

Is desolate of children, strewn with dead,

Sick with a ceaseless moan of stricken things

For ever coming and for ever going,—

Like wild waves darkly driven on a sea

Eternally distress'd."

                       Coldly replied

The goddess, " Take no heed for things of clay,—

For 'twere as well to weep for stricken birds,

Or flowers that in their season fade and fall,

Or beasts that mortals slay for food or cast

Upon thy Father's shrines for sacrifice,

As mourn for that dark dust beneath thy feet

Which thou call'st men. O Balder, take no heed—

Be wise—such pity ill beseems a god !' "

But Balder wrung his hands and wail'd aloud

In a sad human voice, " Not pity *those?*

Hath a bird fallen in my sight and fail'd

To win some meed of tears?   Doth a beast die,

I would not wind in my immortal arms,

And kiss into a new and lovelier life?

And on the dead leaves shed i' the weary woods

Do I not strew my tears divine, like dew?

O Ydun, listen, for thou know'st me not.

The taint of clay is on me and I lack

The large cold marble heart befitting gods.

I drank strange mercy from the dark Earth's breast

When she my foster-mother suckled me

Close to her leafy heart; I am not wise,

Ay me, I am not wise, if not to love

The happy forms below me, and the faces

That love my voice and gladden in my smile,

Be wisdom; I am of them; I have learn'd

The pathos of the setting sun, the awe

Of moonlight and of starlight; nay, I dream

That shape which sets its icy hand on all

Will find me in my season like the rest.

They are my brethren, wanderers in the world,

Yet fatherless and outcast like myself,

And exiled from their home!"

                       But Ydun said,

"That shape which sets its icy hand on all

Need never trouble thee, if thou wilt eat,

Eat as I bid, and live;—nay, Death himself,

Tame as a hound some little child may lead,

Hath fed from out my hand and from my fruits

Drank immortality; and lo, he walks

Immortal among mortals, on Earth's ways

Shedding the sad leaves of humanity.

For this is written, they must die; and those

Who die in battle or with bloody hands

The gods redeem and snatch to deathless days

Of terror in Valhalla; but the rest,

Weak maiden-hearted men and women pale,

And children, dying bloodless, find below

A nameless and an everlasting sleep."

"O Ydun," Balder cried, "I have search'd the Earth,

And have not found him, tho' my spirit pants

To look into his face and question him,
That Death of whom you speak, that fantasy,
Immortal, and a god ; but evermore
His form eludes me in the light and dark,
And evermore beneath my feet I find
Only some gentle shape that he hath slain."

Then Ydun smiled as pallid starlight smiles
On marble, and she answer'd, " Eat then, eat !
And by the gods of Asgard I will swear
To lead thee to him and to read a rune
Which whisper'd in his ear shall make him meek
And weak as any lamb to do thy will ;"
And as she spake she held the apples forth
And proffer'd them again to Balder's lips.

Then hungry for her promise Balder ate,
And in his mouth the mingled red and white
Melted as snow, and suddenly he seem'd
Grown into perfect glory like the moon
Springing all silvern from a summer cloud.

VI.

BALDER AND DEATH.

VI.

BALDER AND DEATH.

I.

THE ALTAR OF SACRIFICE.

"Look!" Ydun said; and pointed.

                         Far in the night

She had led Balder,—o'er the darken'd dales,

And by the silence of black mountain tarns,

And thro' the slumber of primæval woods,—

Till she had come unto an open plain

Cover'd with ragged heath and strewn with stones

As with the broken fragments of some world

Upheaven, rent by earthquake. And the waste

All round was lonely and illimitable,

A tract of stone and heath without a tree,

Save where against the blood-red northern sky

A mountain like the great white hand of Earth

Pointed at highest heaven.   Far out beyond

The shadow of the snowy mountain, rose

Columns gigantic of red granite rock

Scarr'd with the tempest, hung with slimy moss,

And looming in the cold and spectral light

Like living shapes of gods ; and some by storm

Were cast upon the ground and lay full length

Like giants slain, but most stood poised on end,

Not tottering, with their shadows wildly cast

Southward, along the sward.   High in the midst

Stones fashion'd as an altar were upraised,

And on the altar was a coffin'd space

Wherein a man full-grown might lie his length

And with his pleading eyes upon the stars

Make ready for the sacrificial knife.

"Look !" Ydun said ; and Balder look'd ; and saw,

Crouching upon the altar, one that loom'd

Like to a living shape.   And Ydun said,

" That is thy Father's altar, and thereon

Blood-offering brighter than the life of lambs

Is scatter'd by his priests ; at sunset here

A virgin died, and all the desert air
Is sweeter for her breath; and those black birds
That hover o'er the altar moaning low
Are hungry to come near her and to feed,—
But he who lieth yonder hath not fed
His own immortal hunger.   There he broods
Still as a star above her, with one hand
Placed on her lifeless breast!"

                      Then Balder felt
His godhead shrink within him like a flame
A cold wind bloweth, and for pity's sake
His eyes divine were dim; but, creeping close,
Within the shadow of a shatter'd column,
He gazed and gazed.   And lo, the sight he saw
Was full of sorrow only eyes divine
Could see and bear.   Upon the altar-stone
Lay stretchëd naked and most marble white
That gentle virgin, with the slayer's mark
Across her throat, her red mouth open wide,
And two great sightless orbs upraised to heaven
And he who clung unto her, like a hawk

With wings outstretch'd, and dim dilated eyes

Feeding upon the sorrow of her face,

Was he whom Balder o'er the world had sought

And had not found.   Ne'er yet, by sea or shore,

Not ev'n within the silence of the woods

When his sad eyes beheld him first of old,

Had Balder to that spirit terrible

E'er crept so nigh or seen its shape so well.

Shadow it seem'd, and yet corporeal,

But thro' the filmy substance of its frame

The blood-red light of midnight penetrated ;

And dreadfully with dreadful loveliness

The features changed their shining lineaments,

Now lamb-like, wolf-like now, now like a maid's

Scarce blossom'd, now deep-wrinkled like a man's,

Now beautiful and awful like a god's,—

But never true to each similitude

Longer than one quick heart-beat.

                              Thus it hung,

So fascinated by the form it watch'd

It saw not, heard not, stirr'd not, though the birds

Shriek'd wildly overhead.   Ev'n as one cast

Into a trance mesmeric, it prolong'd

The famine of its gaze until its face

Was fixëd as a star.   Then Ydun crept

Close unto Balder, whispering, "Remember

That rune I read thee ! touch him in his trance,

And name him by his mystic human name,

And as I live his lips shall answer thee

In human speech!"   So speaking, Ydun smiled

And vanish'd, leaving Balder all alone

To look and watch and wait. . . .

             . . . Then on his soul,

Beholding that great trance of Death, there came

Most fatal fascination.   For a space

He could not stir.   Upon the sacred grove

Lay darkness ; only on the altar stone

The naked victim glimmer'd beautiful,

And terrible above her linger'd Death ;—

When suddenly beyond the snow-white peak

Rose round and luminous and yellow as gold

The full-orb'd moon ; by slow degrees its beams

Stole down the shrouded mountains, till they fell

Prone on the altar, turning all things there

To brightness :—so that Death himself was changed

From purple into silvern ;—that dead maid

To silvern too from marble ;—the great grove,

With all the columns looming black therein,

New-lit with lunar dawn.   Then as the light

Touch'd and illumed him, for a moment Death

Stirr'd, ev'n as one that stirreth from a sleep,

And trembled, looking upward ; and behold !

His face grew beautiful thro' golden hair,

His eyes dim heavenly blue, and all his looks

Strange and divinely young ! . . .

           . . . Then, ere that trance

Was wholly shaken from him, Balder rose,

And crept unto the altar with no sound ;

And ere the shape could stir or utter cry,

He clutch'd him with one quick and eager hand ;

And tho' his hand was frozen as it touch'd,

Ere Death could fly he gazed into his eyes

And named him by his mystic human name.

. . . And Death gazed back with looks so terrible,

They would have wither'd any living man ;

But Balder only smiled and wove his rune,—

And in a little space the shape was charm'd,

·Looking and listening in a nameless fear.

II.

BALDER AND DEATH.

"O Death, pale Death, thro' many a lonely land
    My feet have follow'd thee ;
Sisters and brothers stricken by thy hand
    Oft have I stoop'd to see :

" To kiss the little children on their biers
    So innocent and sweet,
To bless the old men wearied out with years
    Wrapt in thy winding-sheet.

" To look into thine eyes, to drink thy breath,
    I have cried with a weary cry :
Prayers I have said to the great gods, O Death,
    While thou hast darken'd by.

" Thy mark is on the flower and on the tree,
    And on the beast and the bird,
Thy shade is on the mountains, even the sea
    By thy sad foot is stirred.

"Slayer thou art of all my soul deems fair,
    Thou saddenest the sun,—
Of all things on the earth and in the air,
    O Death, thou sparest none.

"And therefore have I sought with prayers and sighs
    To speak with thee a space!"
Bright Balder in the hollow rayless eyes
    Look'd with a fearless face.

The phantom darken'd 'neath the clay-cold moon
    And seem'd to shrink in woe,
But Balder named his name and wove the rune,
    And would not let him go.

"O Death! pale Death! thou hast a lovelier name,
    Who gave that name to thee?
By the high gods, by that from which they came,
    Thy mouth must answer me!"

Death answer'd not, but mystically bright
    His shadowy features grew,

And on his brow the chilly lamps of night
Sprinkled their glistening dew ;

And Balder wonder'd, for those lights above
Seem'd shining down on him,
And Death's pale face grew as the face of Love,
Yet more divinely dim.

"O Death, pale Death !
Who gave thee that sweet name,
Yet sent thee down to slay poor things of breath,
And turn men's hearts to flame?

"Who gave thee life and cast thy lot below
With those sad slaying eyes?"
Death pointed with a hand as white as snow
Up to the moonlit skies.

"Who sent thee here where men and beasts have
birth?"
Death trembled and was still.
"What drew thee down on my beloved Earth,
To wither up and kill?"

Death answer'd not, but pointed once again

    Up thro' the starry shine ;

And Balder question'd with a quick new pain,

    " My kin ? the gods divine ? "

Death answer'd not, but gazed on Balder now

    With strange and questioning gleam—

His eyes were soft in sorrow and his brow

    Was wonderful with dream.

" Speak to me, brother, if thou art not dumb ;

    Speak to my soul, O Death ! "

The thin lips flutter, but no answer hath come,

    No sigh, no sound, no breath.

Yet on the brow of Death there lives a light

    Like starlight shed on snow,

The fatal face grows beautiful and bright

    With some celestial woe.

And round the shadowy cheeks there softly swim

    Thin, threads of silken hair,

And Balder sees the form world-worn and dim
   Hath once been young and fair.

And as they sit together in the night,
   Hand in hand, mingling breath,
The fingers white of the cold starry light
   Smooth the sad hair of Death.

III.

"O DEATH, PALE DEATH."

"O DEATH ! pale Death !
　　Thy hair is golden, not gray—
In the dark mirrors of thine eyes, O Death,
　　Lie glimmering dreams of day.

" O gentle Death !
　　Thy hand is warm, not chill,—
Thy touch is soft and living, and thy breath
　　Sweet, with no power to kill.

" I love thee, Death, for that great heavenly brow
　　Still dark from love's eclipse—
And lo ! a hundredfold I hunger now
　　To hear thy living lips.

" O gentle Death !
　　Speak, that mine ears may hear."
Then like a fountain rose the voice of Death,
　　Low, sweet, and clear !

IV.

DEATH SINGS.

" I KNOW not whence my feet have come,

Nor whither they must go—

Lonely I wander, dark and dumb,

In summer and in snow.

" For on mine eyes there falls a gleam,

That keeps them dim and blind,

Of strange eternities of dream

Before me and behind ;

" And ever, ever as I pace

Along my lonely track,

The light retires before my face,

Advancing at my back ;

" But ever, ever if I turn

And would my steps retrace,

Close to my back that light doth burn,

But flies before my face.

" I close mine eyes, I fain would sleep,

I rest with folded wing,

Or on my weary way I creep

Like any harmless thing.

" Yet day by day, from land to land,

From gentle fold to fold,

I pass, and lo, my cruel hand

Leaves all things calm and cold.

" Man marketh with his bitterest moan

My shadow sad and dim ;

Of all things hateful, I alone

Am hatefullest to him !

" Ay me, a brand is on my brow,

A fire is in my breast,—

Ever my bitter breath doth bow

Those flowers I love the best.

"I crouch beside the cradled child,
　　I look into its eyes,
I love to watch its slumber mild
　　As quietly it lies.

"I dare not touch it with my hand,
　　Or creep too close to see,
Yet for a little space I stand
　　And mark it, silently.

"Ah, little dream pale human things,
　　At rest beneath the skies,
How, as they sleep, with gentle wings
　　I shade their cheeks and eyes!

"The maiden with her merry laugh,
　　The babe with its faint cry,
The old man leaning on his staff,
　　Are mine, and these must die.

"I touch them softly with my hand,
　　They turn as still as stone,

Then looking in their eyes I stand
    Until their light hath flown.

" I set faint gleams around their lips,
    I smooth their brows and hair,
I place within their clay-cold grips
    The lilies of despair.

" And verily when they bear them forth
    I follow with the rest;
But when their bones are in the earth
    My gentle task is best.

" For there I sit with head bent low
    For many a dreamy day,
And watch the grass and flowers grow
    Out of the changing clay.

" O think of this and blame not me,
    Thou with the eyes divine—
A Shadow creeps from sea to sea,
    Stranger than thine or mine.

" Who made the white bear and the seal ?

The eagle and the lamb ?

As these am I—I live and feel—

 One made me, and I am."

V.

THEN Balder lifted up his voice and cried,

Placing his fingers on Death's heavenly hair,

" Lo, I absolve thee ! " and the Spirit crouch'd

In silence, looking up with wondering gaze

At that immortal brightness blessing him

With holy imposition of white hands.

For beautiful beyond all dream, and bright

Beyond all splendour of the summer Earth,

Divine, with aureole around his head,

God-like, yet fairer far than any god,

Stood Balder, like a thing that could not die !

Upon his face the countless eyes of heaven

Gazed, with their own exceeding lustre dim ;

And moonlight hung around him like a veil

Through which his glory trembled paramount ;

And dim sheen showering from a thousand worlds,

Mingling with moisture of the nether-air,

Touch'd his soft body with baptismal dews.

Then far away in the remotest north,

Cloud-like and dark and scarce distinguishable,

The clustering faces of the gods look'd down..

And Balder cried, " Lo, I have ranged the Earth,

And found it good; yea, hills and vales and streams,

Forests and seas, all good and beautiful ;

And I have gazed in eyes of birds and beasts,

And in the gentle orbs of mortal men,

And seen in all the light of that dim dream

Which grew within my soul when I was born.

Only this thing is bitter, O ye gods,

Most dark and bitter : that eternal Death

Sits by his sad and silent sea of graves,

Singing a song that slays the hopes of men.

Yet lo, I gaze into the eyes of Death,

And *they* are troubled with that self-same dream.

" O gods, on you I cry not, but I cry

On him, the Father, who has fashion'd Death

To be the sorrow of created things,

And set this ceaseless hunger in his heart

To wither up and kill.   Oh, I have wept

Till all my heart is weary, and no voice
Makes answer.   By thy servant Death, O God,
By him whom I have sought and found in pain,
Listen !—Uplift this shadow from the Earth,
And gladly will I die as sacrifice,
And all the gentle things I love shall live."

Far, far away in the remotest north
A white face in the darkness of a cloud
Gleam'd.   Thither, crouching low at Balder's feet,
Death pointed with his skeleton finger fix'd,
Silent.   Then, even as a snow-white lamb
That on the altar cometh with no fear
But looks around with eager innocent eyes,
God Balder on the stone of sacrifice
Leapt, reaching arms up heavenward !

    . . . And he pray'd.

VI.

THE LAST PRAYER.

" FATHER in heaven, my dream is over,

    Father in heaven, my day is dark,—

I sat in the sun and I sang like a lover

    Who sings sweet songs for a maid to mark ;

And the light was golden upon my hair,

And the heavens were blue and the Earth was fair,

And I knew no touch of a human care,

    And I bless'd thy name, my Father !

I sang, and the clarion winds blew clear,

And the lilies rose like lamps on the mere,

And all the night in the balmy light

I lifted up my hands snow-white,

    And the stars began to gather !

" Father, Father, which art in heaven,

    Lord of men and master of Earth.

The rune was woven of colours seven,
  And out of thy being I had birth ;
As a snowdrop wakes on the naked ground,
And opens its eye without a sound
While the winds are murmuring around,
  I woke on the green Earth's bosom ;
And I heard a cry, as the storks went by
Sailing northward under the sky,
And a cry from the mountains answer'd loud,
And the cataract leapt like a corpse from its shroud,
  And the sward began to blossom.

" White clouds passed over with low sweet thunder,
  Shaking downward the silvern dew,
The soft sods trembled and fell asunder,
  And the emerald flame of the grass gleam'd thro',
And the fire of the young boughs overhead
Ran green and amber, golden and red,
And the flashing lamps of the leaves were fed
  At the torch of the flaming sunshine :
Beautiful, wrapt in a blissful dream,
Lay mere and mountain, meadow and stream ;

And beautiful, when the light was low,

Creeping white through the after-glow,

   The starshine and the moonshine !

" Father, Father, hearken unto me,

   Then work thy will on the world and me—

I walk'd the world, and the glad world knew me,

   And my feet were kissed by thy slave the Sea.

And ever with every happy hour,

My love grew deeper for tree and flower,

For the beast in the brake, for the bird in the bower,

   And the deer on the white high places.

But ere my golden dream was done,

I saw thy Shadow across the sun,

I saw thy Shadow that all men see,

On beast and bird, on flower and tree,

   And the flower-sweet human faces !

" The flower-sweet faces of mortal races

   Blossoming sadly under the sky !

I saw my dream on those fading faces,

   I heard my voice in their failing cry.

Out of the soil and into the sun

Their souls were stirring as mine had done,

Their dooms were written, their threads were spun,

   By the hands of the immortals;

They rose in a dream and they lookt around,

They saw their shadows upon the ground,

And wherever they went beneath the blue

The darker Shadow thy Spirit threw

   From the great sun's shining portals.

" Thou hadst taken clay and hadst made it human,

   Blown in its nostrils and lent it breath,

Thou hadst kindled the beauty of man and woman,

   To hunt them down with thy bloodhound, Death.

They did not crave to be born or be,

Yet thou gavest them eyes that their souls might see,

And thou hatest them as thou hatest me

   And the Earth thy godhead bearing.

They shrink and tremble before thy hand,

They ask and they do not understand,

They bid thee pity who pitiest none,

And they name thy name, as I, thy Son,

   Now name it, still despairing.

" Father, Father, which art in heaven,
 Why hast thou fashion'd my brethren so ?
Form'd of fire, with the dust for leaven,
 As thou hast made them, they come and go.
Yet ever thy hand is on their hair
To seize and to slay them unaware,
And ever their faces are pale with prayer
 As round thy fanes they gather. . . .
Thou askest blood and they give thee life
With sweep of the sacrificial knife ;
Thou seekest praise and they give thee pain,
And their altars smoke with the crimson rain
 Thou lovest, O my Father !

" Father, Father, 'tis sad to falter
 Out of the light and into the dark,
Like a wreath of smoke from a burning altar
 To fade and vanish where none may mark.
But O my Father, 'tis blest to be
A part of the joy of the land and sea,
To upleap like a lamb, to be glad and free
 As the stream of a running river.

Could'st thou not spare them a longer space

With sweeter meed of a surer grace ?

Could'st thou not love the light that lies

On happy fields and in human eyes,

    And let it shine for ever ?

" I hear thy voice from the void of heaven,

    It thunders back and it answers ' Nay '—

The rune was woven of colours seven

    For me, thy Son, and for things of clay.

Then mark me now as I rise and swear,

By the beasts in the brake, by the birds in the air,

By Earth, by all those forces fair

    Which mingled in my making,

By men and women who stand supreme

Proud and pale with mine own soul's dream,

I will drink the cup their lips partake !

I will share their lot, while their sad hearts break

    As mine, thy Son's, is breaking !

" Father in heaven, my heart is human,

    I cast a shade like a human thing,

Grant me the doom of man and woman;
 From the Earth I came, to the Earth I cling.
Behold who standeth at my side !
Even Death, thy servant heavenly eyed—
I will die, as the children of men have died,
 To the sound of his sad singing.
Behold, I look in the face of Death,
I look in his eyes and I drink his breath ;
The chill light brightens upon his brow,
He creepeth close and he smileth now,
 His cold arms round me flinging.

" Father, Father, bend down and hearken,
 And place thy hand upon my hair ;
Ere yet I wither, ere yet I darken,
 Hear me murmur a last low prayer.
As the blood of a sacrifice is shed,
Let me die in my brethren's stead—
Let me die ; but when I am dead,
 Call back thy Death to heaven !
Ay me, my Father, if this may be,
I will go with a prayer for him and thee,

I will pass away without a cry,

Blessing and praising thee under the sky,

   Forgiving and forgiven.

" . . . Father, Father, my dream is over—

   He folds me close, and I cannot see ;

Yet I shall sleep like a quiet lover

   If my boon is granted and this may be.

O sweet it is if I may rest

Asleep on my foster-mother's breast,

If over my grave the flowers blow best

   And happy mortals gather.

Yet Father, tho' darkness shrouds my face,

Remember me for a little space,

Remember, remember, and forgive

Thy Son who dies that men may live. . . .

   Accept me, O my Father !"

VII.

THE FIRST SNOWFLAKE—FALLING OF THE SNOW.

He ceased; no voice replied; but round his frame

Cold arms were woven, and his golden head

Droop'd like a lily on the breast of Death. . . .

Then suddenly a darkness like a veil

Was drawn across the silent void of Heaven,

Starlight and moonlight faded mystically,

And save for Balder's face, that as a star

Still flash'd in pallor on the face of Death,

There was no light at all. . . .

　　　　　　　　　　Then Balder cried,

"Lo, he hath answer'd; I am thine, O Death;

Now let me look into thy loving eyes,

And ere I rest, sing low to me again."

Shivering he spake, and sank upon the ground;

But Death stoop'd down above him as he lay,

And took the shining head into his lap,

And smooth'd with fingers cold the silken hair,

And murmur'd Balder's name with singing lips

Soft as the whisper of a wind in June.

"O Death, white Death, all is so cold and dark,

I cannot see the shining of thy face!"

Then touching Balder's lips, Death answer'd low,

" Thy day is ended—thou wilt see no more—

Sleep, sleep!" . . .

. . . But what is this that wavers slowly

Out of that purple blackness overhead?

Is it a blossom from the silvern boughs

O'ershadowing the azure pools of heaven?

Or feather from the plume of some sweet star

That ever moveth magically on

From mansion unto mansion of the sky?

Soft as a bloom from the white hawthorn spray

It wavers earthward thro' the starless dark,

Unseen, unfelt, until it gains the light

Which Balder breathes around him as he lies.

There, as a white moth hovers in the moon,

It floats and gleams, then sinking softly down,

Falls as a seal on Balder's shining brow
And melts away.

"... O Death, upon mine eyes,
And on my brow, I feel a touch like dew,
Like cold dew shaken from a morning cloud.
Look heavenward—seest thou aught of the great gods,
Or God my Father?"   But the form replied,
"On heaven and in the air 'tis night, deep night;
No shape is seen, no star, nor any light.
Sleep, Balder, sleep!"

Then bending low he kissed
The lips of Balder, yea with kisses calm
He drew sweet Balder's breath, and lo! he shone
Brighter and brighter with the life he drank.
But Balder darken'd ever and grew cold.
"O Death, I feel thee smiling in a dream
Serene and still and very beautiful—
But ah, thy lips are chill!" and Death moan'd low,
Winding his thin arms tight round Balder's frame,
"Sleep, sleep!"

. . . O what are these that waver slowly

Out of the purple blackness overhead ?

Soft as that first white blossom blown from heaven,

Faltering downward thro' the rayless dark,

They come, they gather, falling flake on flake

With silvern lapse and silent interchange,

Hovering in soft descent as if they lived.

Upon the drooping head of Death they fall

Like lightly shaken leaves, and looking up

He sees the black air troubled into life

Of multitudinous waifs that wander down.

There is no sound—only the solemn hush

Of mystic motions and invisible wings ;

There is no lamp, no star ; but lo ! the air

Is glimmering dimly with the faint wan light

Shed from the blossoms as they melt and fade.

" Under green boughs, under green boughs, O Death,

Thou hast borne me, and I see not, but I hear

The tremor of the soft trees overhead,

A sound like fountains flowing, and a touch

Like cool leaves shaken on mine eyes and hair ! "

And Balder stirred his gentle head and smiled—
Then drew one last long breath, and sank to sleep.

'Tis over now—the gods may gaze in peace—
Balder is dead !

            Ay me, the light hath passed
From that once glorious head : still as a stone
It lies, not shining, in the lap of Death ;
The hair is white, the eyes are glazed and dim,
There is no red upon the loving lips,
And in its cage the singing heart lies cold.
Ah, Death, pale Death, thy kisses come in vain.
Close thou his lids, and by his side stretch down
The cold white marble arms, and at his head
Watch like a mourner, for a little space.

Death sits and gazes on ; but lo, his looks
Are pale as Balder's. . . . All the light he wore
Hath faded, and his orbs are rayless now.
Lifeless he looms in vigil while his eyes
Turn upward and his thin cold hand still lies

Ev'n as a frozen stone on Balder's heart.

Thicker and thicker from the folds of heaven

The floating blooms are shaken ; lo, the waste

Is with a glittering whiteness carpeted,—

While still o'erhead in ever-gathering clouds,

Drifting from out the vapours of the dark,

The white flakes fall.

          O wonder of the snow !

The world's round ball is wrapt in crystal now,

And out of heaven there comes a freezing breath ;

And nothing stirs or lives ; and in his shroud

Woven by frost's swift fingers, Balder lies,

And that fair face which made creation glad

Is fixëd as a rayless mask of ice.

Crouch at his head, O Death ! and hour by hour

Watch the still flakes of heaven wavering down,

Till thou, and that which lieth at thy feet,

And all the world, are clad in wondrous white !

VII.

THE COMING OF THE OTHER.

VII.

THE COMING OF THE OTHER.

I.

How long he lay in that strange trance of night
  Might Balder never know;
Silently fell the waifs of stainless white,
  And deeper grew the snow.

While out of heaven the falling flakes were shed,
  The dark hours grew to days;
And round and round a red moon overhead
  Went circling without rays.

There were no stars, only that cheerless thing
  Treading the wintry round;
There was no light, save snow-flowers glimmering
  Without a sound.

Darkness of doom is shed on Balder's eyes,
　　But whiteness shrouds the wold;
And still at Balder's head the phantom lies
　　Silent and calm and cold.

And chill is Balder as some naked man
　　Made marble by the frost:
His veins are ice; upon his bosom wan
　　His two thin hands are crost.

But as within some clammy wall of stone
　　The death-watch keeps its chime,—
The cold heart in that crouching skeleton
　　Ticks out the time.

All round, a world of snow, and snows that fall,
　　Flake upon flake, so white;
An empty heaven fluttering like a pall,
　　Lit by that one red light.

All round, the solemn slumber of the snow,
　　No sigh, no stir, no breath,—
But in the midst, scarce audible, slow, low,
　　The throbbing pulse of Death. . . .

The hours creep on, the dreary days are shed,
  Measured by that slow beat ;
And all the while god Balder lieth dead,
  Wrapt in his winding-sheet.

II.

THE LIGHT ON THE SNOW.

O Death, Death, press thy hand so lean and bare
   Upon thy beating heart !
O Death, raise up thy head and scent the air
   With nostrils cold apart !

Awaken from thy trance, O Death, and rise,
   And hearken with thine ears ! . . .
Death stirs, and like a snake with glistening eyes
   His luminous head uprears. . . .

Awaken ! listen !   Far across the night,
   And down the drifts of snow,
There stirs a lonely light,—a blood-red light
   That moveth to and fro.

Small as a drop of dew, most dim to sight,
   . It glimmereth afar. . . .

O Death, it cometh hither,—growing bright
   And luminous as a star.

O Death, pale Death,
   What do thine eyes behold?
What lonely star flasheth afar
   Across the wintry wold?

The world is folded in its shroud of white;
   The skies are smother'd deep;
There is no lamp at all in heaven, to light
   Dead Balder's sleep.

There is no lamp at Balder's head, no star
   Outlooking from the cloud;
White is the snow-drift woven near and far,
   And white is Balder's shroud.

O Death, pale Death, across the lone white land
   No heavenly rays are shed,—
Yet still thou gazest, clutching Balder's hand,
   At yonder gleam blood-red. . . .

It crawleth as a snail along the ground,
    Still far and faint to see,
O Death, it creepeth surely, with no sound,
    Across the night, to thee.

O gentle Death,
    Why dost thou crouch so low?
A star it seems, a star that travelleth
    From snow to snow.

Nearer it cometh, and across the night
    Its beams fall crimson red,
The drifts beneath it glimmer and grow bright
    Like cheeks lamp-lit and dead.

O gentle Death,
    Hither it cometh slow ;—
A Shadow creepeth with the same, O Death,
    From snow to snow.

III.

THE FACE AND THE VOICE.

NEARER and nearer o'er the waste of white
    It steals, and doth not fade:
A light, and in the glimmer of the ligh
    A form that casts a shade.

Nearer and nearer, till Death's eyes behold
    A semblance strange and gray,
A silent shape that stoopeth and doth hold
    The lamp to light its way.

Bent is he as a weary snow-clad bough,
    Gaunt as a leafless tree,
But glamour of moonlight lies upon his brow,
    Most strange to see!

And in one hand a silvern lanthorn swings
    Fill'd with a crimson light,

And round his frame wind-blown and shivering clings
   A robe of starry white. . . .

O Death, pale Death,
   Well may thy cold heart beat !
The form that comes hath piercëd hands, O Death,
   And bloody piercëd feet.

Slowly he crawleth under the cold skies,
   His limbs trail heavy as lead,
Pale fixëd blue his eyes are, like the eyes
   Of one that sleeps stone-dead.

Ay me, for never thro' so wan a wold
   Walk'd one so sadly fair—
The wild snows drift, the wind blows shrill and cold,
   And those soft feet are bare. . . .

O who is this that walketh the wintry night,
   With naked hands and feet !
O who is this that beareth a blood-red light,
   And weareth a winding-sheet !

The night is still, no living thing makes moan ;
  Silent the cold skies loom ;—
But hark ! what voice is this, so faintly blown
  Across the gloom?

" Balder ! Balder ! "
  Hush ! that cry !
The form stands white i' the chilly night,
  Holding its lamp on high.

" Balder ! Balder !
  Where art thou ? "
The snow smooths still with fingers chill
  Dead Balder's brow.

O gentle Death,
  What voice is this that cries ?
What sad shape stands with lifted hands
  Alone under the skies ?

" Balder ! O Balder !
  Answer me ! "

He stands and softly sighs,

And vacant are his eyes

   As if they cannot see !

Yet in the weary gloom full faint they glow,

   And fix themselves at last—

He sees dead Balder sleeping in the snow,

   And thither he fleeteth fast !

He comes now swifter than a bark

   Which bitter tempests blow,—

Dreadful he flashes down the dark,

   With black prints on the snow !

" Wake, Balder ! wake ! "

   His voice calls now—

The shrill cry circles like a snake

   Round Balder's brow !

Oh, who is this that walketh the wintry night

   With naked hands and feet ?

O who is this that beareth a blood-red light

   And weareth a winding-sheet ?

There is a gleam upon his brow and hair
 Ev'n as of luminous hands,
Swiftly he comes to Balder's side, and there
 He stands !

And Death crawls moaning from his snowy seat
 To grasp his raiment hem,
And toucheth with his mouth the piercëd feet,
 Yea, softly kisseth them.

O Death ! pale Death !
 He gazeth down on thee—
His smile is like no smile of thing of breath,
 Yet is it sweet to see.

He lifts the lamp—and lo ! its red rays glance
 On Balder's sleeping eyes—
" Balder ! O Balder ! from thy trance
 Arise ! " . . . .

Strange flash'd the wondrous ray
 Aslant the silent snows ;
Death wail'd—and slowly, gaunt and gray,
 Dead Balder rose !

IV.

"WAKE, BALDER! WAKE!"

Silent rose Balder, ev'n as one
   Who wakens from a swoon,
Turning his head from side to side
   In the red wintry moon.

Wrapt in his winding-sheet of snow
   He loom'd in the dim light,
And marble-pale his cold cheeks gleam'd
   Under his locks of white.

"Wake, Balder! wake!" the strange voice cried;
   Dead Balder woke and heard,
And turn'd his face to his who spake,
   Shiv'ring, but said no word.

"Wake, Balder! wake!" the strange voice cried;
   And Balder woke and knew,—

And lo ! upon his lips and hair

    A golden glimmer grew !

" O who art thou with blessed voice,

    Who biddest my heart beat ?

And wherefore hast thou waken'd me

    From sleep so heavenly sweet ? "

Then answer'd back that tall still form,

    In a clear voice and low,

Stretching his arms and brightening,

    White-robed, and pale as snow.

" I am thine elder Brother

    Come from beyond the sea ;

For many a weary night and day

    I have been seeking thee ! "

Oh, Balder's cheeks are shining bright,

    And smiles are on his face—

" I dream'd, and saw one with a lamp

    Passing from place to place.

" And ever, as he wander'd on,
 Softly he cried to me—
Art thou mine elder Brother ?
 Then shall my lips kiss thee !·"

" I am thine elder Brother,
 Come from beyond the sea ;
Balder, my brother Balder,
 Kiss thou me ! "

Death moans, and crouching on the snow
 Uplooketh with eyes dim,
For Balder on his brother's breast
 Hath fallen, kissing him.

" Thou art mine elder Brother,"
 The risen Balder cries ;
" I know thee by thy gentle voice
 And by thy tearful eyes.

" Thou art mine elder Brother
 Most heavenly sad and sweet,

Yet wherefore hast thou piercëd hands
 And naked piercëd feet?

" O wherefore are thy cheeks so chill,
 Thy lips so cold and blue,
And wherefore com'st thou in thy shroud,
 As if arisen too ? "

The white Christ smiled in Balder's face,
 But softly his tears ran—
" Like thee I lived, like thee I loved,
 And died, like thee, for Man.'

V.

THE BIRTH AND DEATH.

THE white Christ cried, and on the air
   His voice like music rang,
And Balder listen'd silently
   As if an angel sang.

" Out of the dark Earth was I born,
   Under the shining blue,
And to a human height I rose,
   And drank the light, and grew.

" The land was beauteous where I dwelt,
   A still and silent land,
Where little pools of heaven fall
   And gleam 'mid wastes of sand.

" I loved the bright beasts of the earth,
   And birds both great and small ;
I loved all God made beautiful,
   But mortals most of all.

" For on their faces framed of clay,
   And in their eyes divine,
I saw the shadow of the dream
   Which nightly sadden'd mine.

" But when I knew their days were dark,
   And all their spirits sore,
Because of this same silent Death
   Creeping from door to door,

" I raised my hands to heaven and cried
   On him that fashion'd me,
My Father dear who dwells in heaven,
   And suffers Death to be.

" And sweet and low this answer came
   Out of the quiet sky—
All that is beautiful shall abide,
   All that is base shall die !

" *Take thou thy cross and bear it well,*
   And seek my servant Death :
Thou too shalt wither like a flower
   Before his bitterest breath.

" Yea, thou shalt slumber in his arms
    Three nights and days, and then,
With that cold kiss upon thy lips,
    Awaken once again !

"And when thou wakenest at last
    Thy work is yet undone,
For thou shalt roam the Earth, and seek
    Thy Brethren one by one !

" Yea, one by one unto thy heart
    Thy kin shall gather'd be,
Each pallid from the kiss of Death
    And beautiful like thee !"

" O Balder, when my dark day came,
    And in despair I died,
The same sad Death sang low to me,
    Who croucheth at thy side !

" And all my living breath was gone
    For three long nights and days,
And by my side the phantom knelt
    Like one that waits and prays.

" But when my Father's voice again
  Came faint and low to me,
I rose out of my grave, and saw
  Earth sleeping silently.

" He who had hush'd me in his arms
  Was busy other-where. . . .
I stood and watch'd my Father's eyes
  Shine down thro' azure air.

" Then softly, with a happy smile,
  Along the land I crept,
And found the men that I had loved,
  Who waited, lived, and wept.

" And lo, I blessed them one and all,
  And cried with a human cry,
' All that is beautiful shall abide,
  All that is base shall die.'

" But when my loving task was done,
  My soul took better cheer,
And wandering thro' the world unseen
  I sought my Brethren dear.

" All in my robe of snowy white

From realm to realm I trod,

Seeking my Brethren who had died,

The golden Sons of God ! "

VI.

THE PARACLETES.

" I WANDER'D east, thro' shining realms
  Of bright and brazen day,
And there, by a great river's side,
  I saw a Brother pray.

" For past his feet the corpses drave
  Along the yellow tide,
Chased by the emerald water-snakes
  And vultures crimson-eyed.

" And from the banks there rose a wail
  Of women for their dead ;
They wept and tore their linen robes,
  And plunged 'neath wheels of dread.

" Upon his brow he wore a crown,
  But his black feet were bare,

And in his bright and brooding eyes
　　There dwelt a piteous care.

" From his red lips there came a sound
　　Like music of a psalm,
And those who listen'd ceased their tears
　　And grew divinely calm.

" On his own grave he sat and smiled,
　　A spirit dark and sweet,
And there were flowers upon his head
　　And fruits around his feet. . . .

" I wander'd west where eagles soar
　　Far o'er the realms of rains,
And there, among pale mountain peaks,
　　One hung in iron chains.

" His head was hoary as the snow
　　Of that serene cold clime,
Yet like a child he smiled, and sang
　　The cradle song of Time.

" And as he sang upon his cross,
  And in no human tones,
The cruel gods who placed him there
  Were shaken on their thrones.

" I kiss'd him softly on the lips,
  And sighing set him free—
He wanders now in the green world,
  Divine, like thee and me. . . .

" Then faring on with foot of fire
  I cross'd the windy main,
And reach'd a mighty continent
  Wash'd green with dew and rain.

" There swift as lightning in the sun
  Ran beauteous flocks and herds,
And there were forests flashing bright,
  And many-colour'd birds.

" And there the red-skin'd hunters chased
  The deer and wild black kine,—

And lo ! another gentle god
  Was sitting in a shrine !

" His skin enwrought, as if he lived,
  With mystic signs, sat he ;
Shaven his forehead, and his face
  Was painted terribly.

" Yet was he gentle as the dew,
  And gracious as the rain :
With healing gifts he made men glad
  Upon that mighty plain. . . .

" I wander'd south, where rivers roll'd
  Yellow with slime and sand,
And, black against an orange sky,
  I saw another stand.

" Two cymbals held he as he stood,
  And clash'd them with shrill wail :
The clash was as the thunder's voice,
  Heard 'mid the drifting gale.

"Black was his skin as blackest night,
  Naked as night each limb,
Yet in his eyeballs, on his cheeks,
  The heavenly dew did swim. . . .

"O Balder, these thy Brethren were
  Surely as they were mine.
I wander north, and thee I find
  The best and most divine !

"Yea, each of these was offer'd up
  As thou hast been, and I ;
Their blood was drifted ev'n as smoke
  Up to the silent sky.

"All these loved Man and the green Earth
  As thou hast done, and I ;
And each of these by stronger gods
  Was smitten down to die.

"Yet ever when I came, and spake
  The word and made the sign,

Their souls grew clothed in gentleness
  And rose again with mine !

" Yea, for the love of living men
  They stood renew'd in breath,
And smote the great gods from their thrones
  With looks made strong thro' Death.

" With faces fair they rose and wrought
  Against the gods with me,
To make the green Earth beautiful
  From shining sea to sea.

" Yea, Balder, these thy Brethren were,
  Surely as they were mine :
My Father's blessing on thy lips,
  For *thou*, too, art divine ! "

VII.

BENEATH his feet the pale Death crouch'd
 Ev'n as a lean white bear,
Watching with dark and dreamful eyes
 That face so strangely fair.

But paler, sadder, wearier,
 Stood Balder in his shroud,
While overhead a star's still hand
 Parted the drifting cloud;

And from the lattices of heaven
 The star look'd down on him;
But Balder saw not, and his eyes
 With tearful dews were dim.

"O Brother, on my sense still lies
 The burthen of my sleep,
A weight is on me like the weight
 Of winter on the Deep.

" For I remember as I wake .
　Mine old glad life of dream—
The vision of the bridal Earth,
　The glory and the gleam !

" Oh, beautiful was the bright Earth,
　And round her purple bed
The torches of great rivers burnt
　Amber and blue and red !

" And beautiful were living men,
　Wandering to and fro,
With sun and moon and stars for lights,
　And flowers and leaves below.

" But evermore this phantom Death
　Was darkening the sun,
Seeking the sweetest to destroy,
　Sparing and pitying none.

" And lo, I live, and at my feet
　Death cold and silent lies,—

While in thine own dear Father's name
  Thou biddest me arise.

"O wherefore should I rise at all
  Since all is black above,
And trampled 'neath the feet of gods
  Lie all the shapes I love?

" Ay me, the dead are strewn with snows,
  They sleep and cannot see,
With no soft voice to waken *them*
  As thine has waken'd me !

" And wherefore should my soul forget
  What cruel kin were mine,
Tho' in another Father's name
  Thou greetest me divine ? "

The white Christ gazed in Balder's face,
  And held his hand, and cried,
" Divine thou art and beautiful,
  And therefore *must* abide !

" And in mine own dear Father's name
   I greet and bid thee rise,
And we shall stand before his throne
   And look into his eyes."

But Balder moan'd, " Who made the Earth,
   And all things foul or fair?
Who made the white bear on the berg,
   The eagle in the air?

"Who made the lightning's forkëd flame,
   Who thunder's blacken'd brand ?
Who fashion'd Death, with fatal eyes,
   Chill breath, and clammy hand?"

Death stirred and clung to Balder's feet
   And utter'd forth a cry—
A thousand starry hands drew back
   The curtains of the sky !

And countless eyes look'd calmly down
   Thro' azure clear and cold,

And lo ! the round red moon became
  A shining lily of gold !

Then on the wilderness of snow
  A lustrous sheen was shed,
And splendour as of starlight grew
  Around the white Christ's head.

And Christ cried, gazing down on Death,
  Making a mystic sign,
" Now blessings on my servant Death,
  For *he* too is divine.

"O Balder, he who fashion'd us,
  And bade us live and move,
Shall weave for Death's sad heavenly hair
  Immortal flowers of love.

" Ah ! never fail'd my servant Death,
  Whene'er I named his name,—
But at my bidding he hath flown
  As swift as frost or flame.

"Yea, as a sleuth-hound tracks a man,
And finds his form, and springs,
So hath he hunted down the gods
As well as human things!

"Yet only thro' the strength of Death
A god shall fall or rise—
A thousand lie on the cold snows,
Stone still, with marble eyes.

"But whosoe'er shall conquer Death,
Tho' mortal man he be,
Shall in his season rise again,
And live, with thee, and me!

"And whosoe'er loves mortals most
Shall conquer Death the best,
Yea, whosoe'er grows beautiful
Shall grow divinely blest."

The white Christ raised his shining face
To that still bright'ning sky.
"Only the beautiful shall abide,
Only the base shall die!"

VIII.

But Balder moan'd, " O beauteous Earth
　Now lying cold and dead,
Bright flash'd the lamps of flowers and stars
　Around thy golden head !

" And beautiful were beast and bird,
　And lamb and speckled snake,
And beautiful were human things
　Who gladden'd for my sake.

" But lo ! on one and all of those
　Blew the cold blighting breath,
Until I died that they might live
　And bought their life with death.

" Behold, I live, and all is dark,
　' And wasted is my pain,
For glimmering at my feet I see
　The fatal eyes again.

"Why stays he here upon the Earth?
  Why lingers he below?
The empty heavens wait for him,—
  'Tis ended—let him go!"

Death look'd up with a loving face,
  And smiled from the white ground;—
The stars that sat upon their thrones
  Seem'd singing with low sound.

The white Christ cried, "The green Earth lives!
  She sleeps, but hath not died!
She and all fair things thou hast named
  Shall quicken and abide!

"O Balder, those great gods to whom
  Thy radiant life was given,
Were far too frail to keep their plight
  And summon Death to heaven.

"There is no god of all thy kin
  Dare name that name aloud:

When his cold hand was on thy heart,
　Each crouch'd within his cloud.

" Thou couldst not buy the boon of those,
　They were too weak and poor ;
Fain would they buy a boon of *thee*,
　Now thy strange sleep is o'er !

" Yet now for evermore fulfilled
　Is thine ancestral rune,
For thou indeed hast conquer'd Death
　And won thy gentle boon.

" Yea, thou hast died as fair things die
　In earth, and air, and deep,
Yet hast thou risen thrice beautiful
　Out of thy solemn sleep.

" For life thrice seal'd and sanctified
　Is on thy lips and eyes ;
And whatsoe'er grows fair like thee
　By love shall also rise.

" Lo ! out of beauty cast away
    Another beauty grows :
What Death reaps in the fields of life
    In fairer fields he sows.

" And thro' a thousand gates of gloom,
    With tracts of life between,
The creatures that the Father made
    Creep on, now hid, now seen ;

" And duly out of every doom
    A sweeter issue flows,
As out of dreary dooms of gods
    At last thy glory rose !

" So fairer yet, and ever fair,
    Thy soul divine shall gleam,
A spirit springing from a tomb
    And rainbow'd into dream !

" O kiss me, Brother, on the mouth,
    Yea, kiss me thrice again ;

For when I feel thy kiss, I feel

    The sun, and the wind, and the rain !

" The dead Earth wakens 'neath thy feet,

    Flame kindles thro' the sod. . . .

O kiss me with thy human lips,

    Thou brightest born of God ! "

VIII.

THE TWILIGHT OF THE GODS.

VIII.

THE TWILIGHT OF THE GODS.

I.

" Balder ! Balder !"

And Balder said,
Turning round his gentle head,
"I hear ! "

" And thou, my servant Death,
Kneeling low with hushëd breath,
While my hand is on thy hair ! "

Death made answer, kneeling there,
" I hear ! "

" At last the cold snows cease,
The white world is hush'd in peace,

The sky is clear, the storm has gone,
Stars are rising to light us on—
In the north the moon grows gray,—
Take my hand and come away !"

"Whither O whither ?"

"To the City strange wherein
Dwell the mighty gods thy kin ;—
O Balder, lead me thither ! "

" Across the darkness and the day,
Long and dreary is the way—
O'er chill wastes of misery,
Past the silent Frozen Sea,
Where the white bears lean and old
Run and shiver in the cold—
Where the vast ice-mountains rise
Violet-blue against the skies,
Then across the wondrous Bow
Only gods and ghosts may tread,—
Beyond the sea, above the snow,
Where the sunfire fadeth red ;

There the night lies and no day—
Long and weary is the way—
O Brother, fare not thither ! "

" Broken is the wintry night,
Rising yonder is the light ;
Half our task is yet to do—
Come ! and thou, Death, follow too—
O Balder, lead me thither ! "

Far away across the gloom,
Rose-red like a rose in bloom,
Flashing, changing, ray by ray,
Glorious as the ghost of day,
Gleam'd in one vast aureole
Shifting splendours of the pole.
All across the vault of blue
Shooting lights and colours flew,
And the milky way shone there
Like a bosom white and bare,
Throbbing, trembling, softly moved
By some heart that lived and loved.

Night was broken, and grew bright.
All the countless lamps of light
Swinging, flashing, near and far,
Cast their glittering rays below,—
While the silvern polar star
Throbb'd close down upon the snow. . . .

"Take my hand, and let us go!"

II.

AND so those twain have passed across the night,

    O'er frozen wilds of white,

With eyes still fixed upon the polar star

    That burneth bright afar ;

And Death behind them, creeping like a hound,

    Still follows with no sound.

O wonders of the cold untravell'd Waste

    Whereon their swift feet haste !

The night is troubled; on the black pole's pyres

    Flash fierce electric fires,

And shadows come and go, phantoms move forth

    Gigantic in the north.

Upon the snow a green light glimmereth,

    With phosphorescent breath

Flashing and fading; and from unseen lairs
    Creep hoary ghost-like bears,
Crawling across their path without a cry.

    At last against the sky
They see the lonely arctic mountains loom,
    Touch'd with a violet bloom
From peak to base and wearing on their heights
    Strange ever-shifting lights,
Yellow and azure and dark amethyst;
    But westward they are kissed
By the bright beams of a great moon of gold.

    Dead-white and calm and cold
Sleeps the great waste, while ever as they go,
    With shadows on the snow,
Their shapes grow luminous and silvern fair
    And in the hush'd chill air
The stars of heaven cluster with quick breath
    To gaze on them and Death.
Now thro' the trembling sheen of the still sky
    Blue fires and emerald fly

With wan reflections on the sheeted white

    Outspread beneath the night,

And passing thro' them, Christ and Balder seem

    As spectres in a dream,

Until at last their feet come silently

    To the great arctic sea.

Moveless and boundless, stretching blindly forth

    Into the purple north,

Rise mountainous waves and billows frozen all

    As if i' the act to fall,

And tho' they stir not, yet they seem to roll

    In silence to the pole.

So, lit by countless stars, that Ocean old

    Wrapt in the vapours cold

Of its own breath, beneath the lamps of night

    Gleams blue and shadowy white !

Then Balder crieth,—and around his brow

    New glory glimmereth now,—

" Ay me, remote from men are the abodes

    Of the immortal gods ;

Beyond the ocean of the ice ; afar
    Under the sleepless star ;
And o'er the flood of the wild waters spanned,
    From lonely land to land,
By the great bridge of the eternal Bow."

    The white Christ answereth low,
" Tho' it were further than the furthest light
    That glimmereth this night,
Thither our souls are bound, our feet must go !"

.III.

THE BRIDGE OF GHOSTS.

THEIR feet have passed the frozen Deep
    Whose waves in silence roll,
And now they reach that ocean black
    Which beats the inmost pole.

Before them, on the northern sky
    Rose-red and far withdrawn,
Mingled with meteors of the night,
    Gleam golden dews of dawn;

And cast across that liquid sea
    Which surges black below,
They see the pathway of the gods,
    A many-colour'd Bow.

[There comes from off its heights a wind
    That blows for endless time,

As swift as light, as keen as frost,
 It strikes down souls that climb.]

"O brother, place thy hand in mine,"
 The gentle Balder said;
The rayless waters roar'd beneath,
 The Bridge flash'd overhead.

Then hand in hand against the wind
 They falter'd upward slow,
On stairs of crimson and of gold
 Climbing the wondrous Bow.

Like a great rainbow of the earth
 It rose with faint hues seven,
And thro' the purple of the arch
 Glimmer'd the lights of heaven.

When they had reach'd the midmost height,
 In air they stood so high,
To one beneath they would have seem'd
 As stars upon the sky.

The white Christ cried, "What lonely light
    Burns yonder ruby red?"
"The mansion of the sun-god Fryer
    Stands yonder," Balder said.

"There ranged in rows with cold hands crost
    The slain in silence lie,
The face of each ablaze like brass
    Against the burning sky."

Far under, as they linger'd there,
    The dark deep waters roll'd;
Beyond, the polar mountains flash'd
    With gleams of fiery gold.

Upon the shores rose hills of ice
    Hewn as in marble white,
Inlaid with opal and with pearl
    And crown'd with chrysolite.

From stair to stair the brethren trod,
    And Death crawl'd close behind,

And ever as they walk'd, the Bridge
  Shook wavering in the wind.

And lo! they seem'd as meteor shapes,
  White-robed and shod with flame;
And to them out of the cold north
  A threatening murmur came.

Down in the sullen sea below
  Now ghostly faces clomb,
Uplooking with wild eyes to theirs
  And waving hands of foam!

So o'er the mighty Bow they moved
  Snow-vestured and star-crown'd,
And Death behind them like a shade
  Follow'd without a sound.

But as they reach'd the shores and stood,—
  The bright Bridge at their back,—
The gods gazed out from the cold north
  And shriek'd, and all grew black!

Deep thunders shook the darken'd heaven,
 Wild lightning flash'd and fled,
The frozen shores of ice and snow
 Trembled beneath their tread.

Round the ice-mountains of the pole
 Dense smokes of tempest rose,
And from their lairs swift whirlwinds leapt
 Wrapt round with drifting snows.

"O Brother, hold me by the hand,
 For lo ! the hour is nigh ;—
I see the shadows of the gods,
 Yonder upon the sky ! "

IV.

"BEHOLD, I AM RISEN."

THEY stood in the snow and they clung together,—
  The air was blacken'd, the snow was driven;
There came a tempest of wintry weather
  Out of the open gates of heaven.
The darkness drifted, the dark snows shifted,
The winnowing fans of the winds were lifted,
  And the realms of the ice were riven;
The white flakes whirl'd like a wingëd cloud
  Round and over and under;
The Earth shriek'd loud from her rending shroud,
  And the black clouds echoed in thunder!

"O Balder! Balder!"

                    And Balder replied,
Feeling not seeing his face who cried,
"I hear!"

" And thou other who crouchest there,
Gazing up thro' thy hoary hair,
　Stir not yet till I bid thee go ! "

And Death moan'd answer out of the snow,
" I hear ! "

" At last the hour hath come,
The sky is troubled, the world is shaken,
The sleeping gods on their thrones awaken,
　Altho' their lips are dumb.
I feel a breath from the frozen north,
For the souls of the slain are faring forth,
And their tramp is heard on the frozen ocean,
　And their tread is swift in the vales of snow.
　They come, and the great deep throbs below
To the sound of their thund'rous motion.
O Balder, Balder ! "

　　　　　" I hearken, I hearken ! "

" Thro' the flakes that fall and the ways that darken,
Over the earth or over the sea,
North is the way that our feet must flee,

Till we find them sitting beyond the pole,

Gods without pity, gods without soul,

   Fresh from the slaying of thee.

North is the way that our feet must go,

Breasting the blasts from the gates of woe,

Till we find them there in their sacred places,

Gods with their terrible bloodless faces,·

Writing red-handed for mortal races

   Black runes on the stainless snow !'

. . . Deeper and darker the night is growing,

Faster and faster the clouds are snowing—

Fleeter and fleeter the Brethren fly

With faces silver'd against the sky,

Till close before them, beyond the pole,

The aurora flashes its fiery scroll,

While the winds of the frozen waste are blowing,

   And the ice is riven asunder !

Lo ! ghastly blue with a dreary gleam

The bergs of the pole, like ghosts in a dream,

Standing pallid against the heaven,

Flash with the forks of the fiery levin,

And to and fro in the frozen snow,

  Pass manifold shapes of wonder.

Faster, faster, out of the north,

The ghosts of Asgard are hurrying forth,

And their shields of ice and their spears of hail

Clash in the heart of the gathering gale,

  As they come upon feet of thunder.

"O Balder! Balder! cling unto me!"

"Lift up thy lamp, for I cannot see—

I shiver deep to the bitter bone,—

While the chilly seeds of the sleet are sown

  In my flesh, and I feel not thee!"

The lamp is lifted : a dreary light

It sheddeth out on the northern night ;

It comes and goes like the lighthouse ray

Lost on the soot-black ocean way.

Nought they see and nought they feel,

Only the frost with fingers of steel

Gripping their throats, so fierce, so fast,

Only the breath of the bitter blast

Bending their bodies as trees are bent,
Rending their garment as clouds are rent,
While overhead, with a thund'rous tread,
The black heavens frown to trample them down,
  And the vials of storm are spent.

"O Balder! Balder! what shadows white
Stand in the tempest's shrieking flight?
There in the darkness I discern
Faces that fade and eyes that burn;
They loom in the flash of the thunder-cloud,
And the tramp of their feet is as surges that roar,
Rolling aloud,
  On some desolate rocky shore."

Then Balder answer'd with eager cry—
"Cover thy face lest thou droop and die:
'Tis the gods my brethren! I see them plain,
Each sitteth there in a spectral pain;
They search the waste all round for us,
And the light in their eyes is tremulous
  With the wrath that burns the brain!"

. . . Blacker, blacker, the night is growing,

Thicker, faster, the snow is snowing.

Silent amid those frozen peaks

Sit gods with terrible bloodless cheeks,—

Each like a statue of marble stone,

Each alone on a lonely throne,

With the red aurora upon their hair,

They loom in desolate circle there,

 Silent, with folded wings ;

They do not stir though the storm drifts by,

They do not speak though the wild winds cry,

Silent they reign in a starry dream,

While the north star flashes its fiery beam

 And the serpent lightning springs. . . .

Silent they sit,—but who is He

Who broods in the centre awfully ?

Like a pale blue berg in the frosty light,

Solemn, speechless, hoary white,

Coldly wrapt from head to feet

In a robe of snow like a winding-sheet,

With a crown of starlight on his hair,

He sitteth dreaming with fatal stare,

Tho' his throne is strangely shaken.

Black is his throne, and he sits thereon

Stil as a mortal whose breath is gone,

And the waves are frozen around his feet,

And faint, far under, the earthquakes beat,

Yet he broods, and doth not waken.

"O Balder ! Balder ! who is he

Who sitteth there so silently ?

Who sitteth there so hoary and old,

A god in the midst of gods so cold,

And hears not at all, though the storm winds call,

And the ghosts of Asgard gather ? "

Then Balder answer'd, " The gods creep here,

Weary with seasons of strife and fear—

They come, they go—but for ever and aye

He stirreth not, be it night or day ;

Still as a stone, he reigneth alone ! "

And Balder raising his hands, made moan,

"BEHOLD I AM RISEN, MY FATHER !"

V.

ALFADUR.

THE rune is woven, the spell is spoken,
And lo ! the dream of the gods is broken,
  And each pale throne is shaken.
They rise, they tremble against the sky,
They shriek an answer to Balder's cry
  And white as death they waken !
Gods they glimmer in frozen mail,
Their faces are flashing marble pale,
They rise erect, and they wave their hands,
They scatter the shifting snows as sands,
  And gaze in the face of the Father ! . . .

. . . Blacker, blacker, the night is growing,
Faster, faster, the snow is snowing—
Silently looming thro' the storm,
Towers the one gigantic Form,

And all around with a trumpet sound
The wintry winds are blowing.
The light of doom is in his eyes, his arms spread wide
for slaughter,
He sits 'mid gleams of burning skies and wails of wind-
blown water,
Behind the outline of his cheeks the pale aurora
flashes,
He broods 'mid moveless mountain peaks and looks
thro' fiery lashes :
On heaven and earth that round him float in whirls of
snowy wonder,
He looks, and from his awful throat there comes the
cry of thunder !

"BALDER ! BALDER !"

. . . "He cries on me—
He standeth yonder, and beckoneth !"
"He looketh around, but he cannot see !
Answer him back with a gentle breath,
Now the air is still !" . . .

"I am here, I am here !"

. . The cry went up to the godhead drear,

Like the cry of a lamb in the midst of the snow,

When the voices of tempest have sobbed their fill,

  And the clouds are still

For a little space, and the winds lie low.

Then rose in answer a wail so loud

It roll'd as thunder from cloud to cloud,

And the gods arose in a wingèd crowd,

As oft 'mid desolate mountain-peaks,

With clangour of wings and hungry shrieks,

  Great flocks of eagles gather.

Tearing asunder their frozen mail,

Smiting their breasts with a woful wail,

Looming with faces spectral pale,

  They gazed in the eyes of the Father !

Then even as mighty eagles spread

Their wings and soar, they arose and fled !

Crossing the gleam of the fiery north,

Facing the dark drift hurrying forth,

  They flew on flashing pinions ;

As wild clouds scatter'd across the sky,

They wing'd their way with a thunder-cry. . . .

But moveless there, when the rest had flown,

The Father sat on his silent throne,

Dreary, desolate, all alone,

In the midst of his white dominions.

" Balder ! Balder !"

" He looks on me !

He stirreth now, with a sound like the sea,

And he calleth aloud !"

" Then move no limb,

But crouch in thy place and answer him ;—

Cry once more full loud and clear,

Now he pauseth again !" . . .

"I am here, I am here !"

Again the thunder rolling near,

Again the tumult of wind and ocean ;

Around the throne with a serpent motion

The meteor snakes appear.

White in the midst He stands, the Spirit of God the

Master,

Waving his wild white hands, urging his snows on
    faster ;
But ever darker yet the troubled air grows o'er him,
And still with fierce face set he searcheth night before
    him,
And then again, all blind, with black robes blown
    asunder,
He gropeth down the wind, and calls aloud in thunder,

        " BALDER, BALDER."

        . . . " I see him now,
The wrath of heaven is on his brow—
He stands in the circle of meteors white,
His white feet glimmer like cold moonlight—
I can feel his breath ! "

            " Now hold my hand—
Rise erect on thy feet and stand—
Make answer ! "

             " My Father, I am here ! "

As an infant's cry, so faint, so clear,
As a young lamb's cry, so soft, so low,

Cometh the voice from the waste of snow,—

And silence deep as the sleep of ocean,

Stillness with no stir, no motion,

  Follows the sound of the cry. . . .

Terrible, desolate, the Form

Stands and broods in the midst of the storm,

Beneath him wolves of the fierce frost swarm,

  But quiet and hush'd they lie.

With his robe wind-rent and his form wind-blown

  He gazeth round and round.

He seeth a snow amid the snow

  And heareth a human sound.

"BALDER! BALDER!"

        "O Father dear,

Turn thine eyes and behold me here—

Ev'n Balder thy Son!"

        "*I see thee not—*

Only a gleam on a darken'd spot,

And the ray of the light in thy hand!"

"Ay me,

No light I carry that thou mayst see.

What wouldst thou, Father?"

    " Why hast thou risen?

We deem'd thee dead, and we slept in peace—

We deem'd thee dead with the snow for prison,

 That the old sad fear might cease.

We deem'd thee dead, and our hearts were light,

For nevermore would thy beauty blight

   The spirit of Me thy Father!"

Then answer'd Balder, "O Father dear,

Turn thine eyes, and behold me here—

Why hatest thou me?"

    " We hate thee all

For thy summer face, for thy soft footfall,

For thy beauty blended of star and flower,

For thine earthly love, for thy heavenly dower;

For the rune that was written, the rune that was read,

We cursed thee all, but our curse was said

Deepest and best when we read that rune

By thy love for men!"

As the rising moon

Creeping up from a cloudy place,

A glory grew upon Balder's face—

Again he murmur'd, "O Father dear,

Turn thine eyes and behold me here—

Why hatest thou me?"

"We hate thee most

By the rune that was written, the rune that was lost,

By the doom that above thee hung sharp as a sword,

When thy feet stood there and thy voice implored

For pity of men; and we loved thee least

For loosing the yoke of man and beast,

For making the hearts of mortals tame,

For calming wild hawk-like men who came

To thy beck as doves; then we loathed to see

The light of thy name upon flower and tree,

The peace of thy name upon hill and vale,

The love of thy name on the faces pale

Of maidens and men; yea, for all these things,

For all thy life and the light it brings,

We have hated and hate thee unto death."

But Balder answereth back and saith,
" Why hatest thou me ? "

" For this the most !
Because thy coming is as the ghost
Of the coming doom that shall strike us dead.
For the rune was written, the rune was read,
And we knew no rest till we bought our breath
With the gentle boon of thy willing death.
Why hast thou risen ? how hast thou risen ?
We gave thee the frost and the snow for prison,
We heard thy sigh and we let thee die,
Yet thou criest again with a human cry
From the gates of life ! . . . But I stoop at last
To sweep thee hence with my bitterest blast
Out to the heavens of pitiless air,
Where nevermore with a human care
That face of thine
May trouble the eyes of the gods divine !
Out 'mong the wingëd stars, deep down the dark abysses,
Beyond the black tomb's bars, far from the green Earth's
kisses,

As dust thou shalt be cast, as snow thou shalt be drifteo

Seized by my fiercest blast thou shalt be now uplifted.

Call on all living things that stir in sun or shadow—

White flowers, sweet forms with wings, wild deer, o:
>   *lambs o' the meadow ;*

Call on the moonlight now that mingled in thy making

To heaven uplift thy brow, where the pale spheres ar
>   *waking ;*

On water, air, and fire, on snow and on wind and o:
>   *forest,*

Call with a wild desire, now when thy need is sorest !

Call now on flower or bird to fill the plight they gaɪ
>   *thee !*

Call, let thy voice be heard, and see if Earth can sav
>   *thee !*"

> Behind the back of the Shadow hoar,
> There grew a trouble, a sullen roar,
> Roar as of beasts that prepare to come,·
> Trouble like surges that flash to foam;
> Faster and faster the drift whirl'd round
> Deeper and direr grew the sound,

And the four fierce winds are blowing !
Yet brighter, calmer grew Balder's face,
Till a light and a glory fill'd the place,
And he rose his height, like a lily white,
Like a lily white in the heart of the night,

   With the flakes around him snowing !

VI.

THE BRETHREN.

" FATHER, Father, why hatest thou me,

Whom the green Earth loves, and the circling sea,

And the pure blue air, and the light of the sun,

And the birds of the air, and the flowers each one?

Hatest thou me thro' my love for these?

For the swift deep rivers, the fronded trees,

The golden meres and the mountains white,

The cataracts leaping from height to height,

And the deer that feed on the snowy steeps

Where the rainbow hangs and the white mist creeps i

Hatest thou me the most of all

For my care of mortals whom thou hast made,

My blessing on lovers whose soft footfall

Soundeth still in the flowery shade?

Father, Father, hatest thou me,

Because of my light on humanity?

Because with a holy anointing balm

I have heal'd their hearts and kept them calm;

Because I have sown in forest and grove

The roses of beauty, the lilies of love,

That men might gather, and sweeten away

The taint of the perishable clay?

Father, Father, listen to me—

I will not call upon bird or tree,

I will not call upon lamb or dove,

On the flowers below or the stars above;

I will call aloud, and thine ears shall know,

I will call aloud in the midst of the snow,

On a mortal thing of mortal breath

Who has gazed and smiled in the eyes of Death,

Who has loosen'd his shroud and his feet made
    free

To follow and find me over the sea.

   . . . . My brother Jesus, hearest thou me!"

Sweet as a star that opens its lids of silver and
    amber,

Soft as a lily that rises out of a water still,

Pure as a lamp that burns in a virgin's vestal
    chamber

  When winds with folded wings sleep on the scented
    sill,

Pale as the moving snow, yet calmer, clearer, and
    whiter,

  Holding the light in his hand, and flashing a ray
    blood-red,

Robed in a silvern robe that ever grew stranger and
    brighter,

  Robed in a robe of the snow, with a glory around
    his head,

Christ now arose! and upstanding held the cold
    hand of his Brother,

  Turning his face to the storm like the wrath of
    some beautiful star,—

And the sound of the storm was hush'd, and pale
    grew the face of that Other,

  He, Alfadur supreme, most direful of all gods that
    are !

  " BALDER ! BALDER !"

"O Father, I listen!"

"What shape is this whose sad eyes glisten

Bright as the lamp he is uplifting?

Round and o'er him snows are drifting,

Yet as a still star shineth he,

Pale and beautiful like thee.

Who is this that standeth there

Even as a mortal man,

Thin and weary and wan,

A lanthorn in his hold,

His feet bloody and bare,

And a ring of brightest gold

　　Round his hair?"

"O Father, 'tis he and none other

　Who woke me from my tomb;

The Christ it is, my Brother,

　Tho' born of a woman's womb.

He has conquer'd the grave, for lo!

　He died and he rose again!

He comes to the silence of snow

　From the beautiful regions of rain;

And his hair is bright with a peaceful light
As the yellow moon's on a summer night,
And the flesh on his heart is heapen white
    To cool an immortal pain ! "

Blacker, blacker the night is growing,
Deeper, deeper the snow is snowing. . . .
As the rigid wave of the ocean-storm
Towereth the gigantic Form,
And he lifts his hand with a cold command,
    And the shrill winds answer blowing !
A ghastly gleam is on his cheeks, his white robes roll
    asunder,
He raises up his arms and shrieks in his old voice of
    thunder,
" *The rune was writ, the rune is read—Son, thou hast
    slain thy Father,*
*The frames are quick that late were dead, and from the
    grave they gather,*
*The pale One cometh heavenly eyed, as in thy dreams,
    O Mother !*
*He wakes, he stands by Balder's side as brother smiles
    by brother.*

O gods, these live, and must we die? these bloom, and
    must we wither?

Cry with a loud exceeding cry on Death and send him
    hither!

Come, come, O Death! I call on thee—come hither,
    fleeter, faster!

Thou hunter of humanity, thou hound of me thy
    Master!

Slay thou these twain, that we may live, who feed thy
    throat with slaughter,

And blood to quench thee gods will give, shed free as tor-
    rent water!

Come thou this night, O Death divine, come quickly or
    come never,

And the great Earth shall all be thine for ever and for
    ever!"

    The snows are blowing, the Earth is crying,

    The eagles of storm are shrieking and flying;

    Thunder-cloud upon thunder-cloud

    Piled, and flashing and roaring aloud,

    Roll from the north, and the winds rush forth,

      And the billows of heaven are breaking.

Hand in hand the Brethren stand,

Fair and bright in the midst of the night,

Fair and bright and marble white,

  Quiet as babes awaking. . . .

But who is *he* that stirring slow,

Wrapt in winding-sheet of snow,

Riseth up from the Christ's feet?

His golden hair all white with sleet,

His eyes all dim, his face snow-pale,

He stands erect in the drifting gale !

Tall and terrible loometh he,

Facing the blast like a frozen tree !

" *Death, Death !*" the god shrieks now—

Death, Death, is it surely thou?

Death, Death !" and the god laughs loud,

Answer'd by every thunder-cloud,

  While the snows are falling faster,—

" *Death, Death, there is thy prey !—*

Take them and tear them and rend them away,

As flakes of snow, as drops of spray,

  In the name of Me thy Master !" . . .

Like two lilies crown'd with gold,

Very beauteous to behold,

   Blown in summer weather,

Like two lambs with silvern feet,

Very beauteous and sweet,

Held together with a chain

In some sacrificial fane,

   The Brethren cling together.

Ever fairer still they grow

While the noise of storm sinks low,

And the Father's snow-white hand

Pointeth at them as they stand,

And the silent shape of Death

Creepeth close and shuddereth !

See, O see, the light they wear,

On their heads and o'er their hair,

Falleth on the Phantom now,

Lying softly on his brow. , . .

Death, O Death, can this be *thou ?*

19

VII.

FATHER AND SON.

Now hark, one crieth!

        " My servant Death,

Kneeling there with hushëd breath,

Listen, ere I bid thee go!"

Death makes answer out of the snow,

" I hear!"

      The Christ hath risen his height,

Large and strange in a lonely light,

And he lifts his hand and makes the sign

Of the blessed cross on his breast divine,

And the thrones of the white gods flash like fire,

And sink in earthquake around the Sire,

   Shaken and rent asunder!

Then he lifts his hand and he makes the sign

Once again on his breast divine,

And the mountains of ice around the throne
Are troubled like breakers rolling on
　To the sound of their own thunder!

"Father! Father!" Balder cries,
With arms outstretch'd and weeping eyes,
"Father!"—but lo! the white Christ stands,
Raising yet his holy hands,
And cries, "O Death, speed on! speed on!
Conquer now and take thy throne—
Now all the gods have taken flight,
Reign thou there one starless night
　In the room of him, the Father!"

Slowly over the icy ground,
Slow and low like a lean sleuth-hound,
Without a breath, without a sound,
　The phantom form is crawling.
He makes no shadow, he leaves no trace,
Snow on snow he creepeth apace,
Nearer, nearer, the fixëd Face
　Veil'd with the flakes still falling.

"Father! Father!" Balder cries . . .

Silent, terrible, under the skies,

Sits the God on his throne, with eyes on his Son

   Whose gentle voice is calling!

As the cuckoo calls in the heart of the May

   Singing the flowers together,

As the fountain calls thro' its flashing spray,

As a lamb calls low 'mid a mountain-cloud,

As a spirit calls to a corpse in its shroud,

   The Son cries on the Father!

VIII.

TWILIGHT.

THE wind is blowing, the skies are snowing,
  The ice is rent and the rocks are riven,
But morning light in the north is growing,
  Crimson light of the altars of heaven.
Silent, still, amidst the storm,
Sitteth there the formless Form,
Hearkening out of his hoary hair,
Waiting on in a dark despair,
  While the burning heavens flame o'er him ! . . .
Suddenly, wild and wing'd and bright,
Towering to heaven in shroud of white,
A phantom upriseth against the light
  And standeth vast before him. . . .
Is it a shadow, or only the snow ?
The skies are troubled, the light burns low,
  But stars still gather and gather.

Is it a Shadow, or only the snow,

Uprising there in the blood-red glow,

Ever towering higher and higher,

In a robe of whiteness fringed with fire,

Outstretching wings without a cry

From verge to verge of the burning sky,

　　With eyes on the eyes of the Father?

Now Balder crieth, "What shape comes there,

Terrible, troubling the heavens and air?

Is it Norna the arctic swan,

The bright and bodiless Skeleton,

Bird-shaped, with a woman's breasts and eyes,

Whose wings are wide as the world and skies?

Is it Norna, or only the snow,

Moving yonder against the glow,

Ever towering higher and higher,

Ever outspreading pinions dire

And looking down in a dumb desire,

　　With eyes on the eyes of the Father!"

It is not Norna, it is not the snow.

The skies are troubled; the light burns low;

　　Yet stars still gather and gather.

"Father! Father! awaken, awaken!

One bends above thee with bright hair shaken

Over thy throne like a falling flame;

One toucheth thy cheek and nameth thy name,

In a voice I hear, in a tone I know;

It is not Norna, it is not the snow,

   By the face and the voice and the tone.

Vaster than these and vaster than thou,

Touching the stars with a shining brow,

Flickering up to the twinkling shades

Where the wild aurora flashes and fades,

Spreading its wings from east to west,

As an eagle that looks on a hawk in its nest

   It hungereth over thy throne!

Father! my Father!"

                " He cannot hear—

Hide thy face, for the hour is near—

Hush!" . . .

   . . . Who shrieks in the heart of the night? . . .

Terrible, desolate, dumb and blind,

   Like a cloud snow-white

Struggling and rent in the claws o' the wind,

The Father hath risen with no sound

'Mid the wild winds wavering around,

And his stirring deepens the storm.

The ice is shaken beneath his tread,

The meteors burn around his head,

But faster, thicker, out of the skies,

Blotting his shape from Balder's eyes,

The wild flakes waver and swarm.

Now face to face in the blood-red gleam,

Like clouds in the sunset, like shapes in a dream,

Face to face, with outstretch'd hands

Like lightning forks that illume the lands,

Face to face, and sight to sight,

Like vulture and eagle fierce for fight,

They rise and they rise against the skies,—

Alfadur with his fiery eyes,

And the other vaster Form !

It is not Norna, but stranger and brighter,

It is not the snow, but wilder and whiter ;

Ever greater yet it grows
Wrapt about with whirling snows,
Ever it dilateth on,
Till, a crimson Skeleton,
With his head against the sky
Where the pale lights flicker and die,
Strange, he stands, with orbs of fire
Looking down upon the Sire.
See O see upon his brow
Strangest lustre liveth now,
On his neck and round his frame
Twines a snake of emerald flame. . . .
Death, O Death, can it be *thou?*

" Father, father ! I cannot see—
The heavens are bright, but the world is white,
The wings of the wan Form cover thee—
Around and around, with no sigh, with no sound,
Like the mists of a cloud, like the folds of a shroud,
  They enwrap thee,—and hide thee from me ! "

IX.

"A CROSS AND A LILY."

" IT is over ! O Balder, look up and behold ! "

" Not yet, for I sicken—my sense shrinketh cold,

And I fear the strange silence that cometh at last !

All is hush'd—all is dead—the dew now is shed

Warm as tears on my hand, but the tempest hath
    pass'd,

    And the sounds of the tempest are fled ! "

" Arise ! "

        " I am risen ! "

                " Behold ! "

                        " All is white,

But the darkness hath gone, and the stars of the night,

And down from the north streams the dawn flowing
    free ;

But I see not my Father! "

                " Again ! "

                        " Woe is me !

His throne standeth there white and cold, and thereon
Sits another I know, as a King on a throne,
Yea, sceptred and crownèd . . . and vaster tenfold
He seems than the Spirit who sat there of old,
For his form 'gainst the heavens looms fiery and fair,
And the dew of the dawn burneth bright on his hair ;
And we twain unto *him* are as birds in the night
That sit gazing up at a great snowy height
Where the starlight is coming and going like breath."

"So strange and so changed, yet 'tis he, even Death,—
Best and least, last and first.   He hath conquer'd his
   own.
All gods are as sand round his feet tempest-blown,
And lesser yet greater, more weak yet more wise,
Are we who stand here looking up in his eyes.
All hail now to Death, since the great gods are dead !"

" Woe is me—it was written, and lo ! it is read ! "

" Come together, and bless him ! "

               " My Father ? "

                    " The same.

On his throne I will mark with a finger of flame
A cross and a lily for thee and for me ! "

They pass o'er the ice, and a sound like the sea
Grows under their footprints ; and softly they come
Where Death, with his eyes fix'd on heaven, sitteth
    dumb ;
And they pause at his feet, while far o'er them he
    looms
With his brow 'mong the stars and the amethyst
    glooms,
Yea, they pause far beneath, and with finger divine
The white Christ hath made on the snow for a sign
The cross and the lily . . . then rising he stands,
And looketh at Death with uplifting of hands.

Still as a star he shineth, brightly his eyes are burning,
    White as a dove he seems in the morning's dewy
      breath,
Lifting again his face with a smile of loving and
      yearning,
    He looketh gently up at the godlike shape of Death;

And the hair of Death is golden, the face of Death
    is glowing,
    While softly around his form he folds his mighty
      wings,
And vast as the vast blue heavens the fair faint form
    is growing,
    But the face that all men fear is bright with beautiful
      things.
Ev'n so the Brethren wait where the darkest snows
    are drifted, .
    Small as two doves that light in a wilderness alone,
While bright on the blood-red skies, with luminous
    head uplifted,
    In a dream divine upgazing, Death sitteth upon
      his throne.

IX.

THE LAST BLESSING.

IX.

THE LAST BLESSING.

I.

THE WAKING OF THE SEA.

" ALL that is beautiful shall abide,
  All that is base shall die."
Hark ! birds are singing far and wide,
  Under the summer sky. . . .

Southward across the shining Bow
  The blessed Brethren came ;
They wore soft raiment of the snow
  And sandals shod with flame.

And golden lights and rippling rains
  Were on the frozen sea,
The bergs were melting from their chains,
  The waters flashing free.

The white Christ lifted hands above
  That silent wakening Deep;
And the unseen depths began to move
  With motions soft as sleep.

Then on an isle of ice he stept,
  Leading his Brother mild,
And blest the waters as they slept,
  And lo, they woke and smiled !

Around him on the melting sea
  The glittering icebergs stirred,
And glimmer'd southward silently,
  Like things that lived and heard.

Then, like a ship on the still tide
  That slowly leaveth land,
His own white isle began to glide
  At lifting of his hand.

Silently as a flock of sheep
  The bergs stirred in the sun,
Shepherded gently down the Deep
  By that immortal one.

For as he raised his snow-white hand,
　　They crept full softly by,—
Or paused and stood, as fair flocks stand
　　Under the shepherd's eye.

Far, far away into the north
　　They stretch'd in legions white,
Trembling and changing, creeping forth
　　Out of a crimson light.

And all the colours of the Bow
　　Down their bright sides were shed ;
Above the sky was gold ; below,
　　The sea all rippling red !

II.

FROM DEATH TO LIFE.

BRIGHT Balder at his brother's feet
　　Lay looking on the sea,
And sea-birds hover'd white and sweet
　　Around him, silently.

And white bears crawl'd out of the Deep
　　To see him, and were blest ;
And black seals with their young did creep
　　Upon the berg to rest.

Brighter and fairer all around
　　The kindling waters shone ;
And softly, swiftly, with no sound,
　　The white flocks glided on.

And far away on every side
　　The glittering ice-blink grew,—
Millions of bergs like ships that ride
　　Upon the waters blue.

"O Balder, Balder, wherefore hide
  Thy face from the blue sky!"
The voice was music, but it cried
  Like any human cry.

" O Balder, Balder," the white Christ said,
  "Look up and answer me."
Bright Balder raised his golden head,
  Like sunrise on the sea.

" O Brother, I was weeping then
  For those whom Death o'erthrew.
Shall I, whose eyes have mourn'd for men,
  Not mourn my brethren too?"

The white Christ answer'd back, and cried,
  Shining under the sky,
" All that is beautiful shall abide,
  All that is base shall die.

" And if among thy sleeping kin
  One soul divine there be,
That soul shall walk the world and win
  New life, with thee and me.

" Death shall not harm one holy hair,
   Nor blind one face full sweet;
Death shall not mar what Love made fair;
   Nay, Death shall kiss their feet !"

Then Balder rose his heavenly height,
   And clear as day smiled he ;
His smile was bright as noonday light
   Upon the sparkling sea.

Turning his face unto the north,
   He utter'd up a prayer,
He saw the great Bridge stretching forth,
   But never a god walk'd there.

He pray'd for those great gods o'erthrown
   And cast in Death's eclipse,
He named the goddesses each one,
   And blest them with his lips.

And lo ! from bright'ning far-off lands
   He saw glad spirits gleam,
Gazing to sea, and waving hands,
   And singing in a dream ;

And far away where earth and air
   Mingled their gentle lights,
There stood one marble form most fair
   Upon the cloudless heights.

Against the calm and stainless blue
   It stood divinely dim,
And lo, his mother's form he knew,
   And felt her eyes on him !

Silent she paused, serene and crown'd,
   Amid a summer sheen,
And cataracts flash'd their lights around,
   And woods grew dewy green.

Softly he sail'd beyond her sight
   Upon the summer sea,
And once again with hands snow-white
   He blest all things that be.

And brighter, brighter, as he blest,
   The loosen'd Ocean grew,
And all the icebergs rock'd at rest
   Upon the waters blue.

Along the melting shores of earth
  An emerald flame there ran,
Forest and field grew bright, and mirth
  Gladden'd the flocks of Man.

Then glory grew on earth and heaven,
  Full glory of full day !
Then the bright rainbow's colours seven
  .On every iceberg lay !

In Balder's hand Christ placed his own,
  And it was golden weather,
And on that berg as on a throne
  The Brethren stood together !

And countless voices far and wide
  Sang sweet beneath the sky—
" All that is beautiful shall abide,
  All that is base shall die ! "

THE END.

Hazell, Watson, and Viney, Printers, London and Aylesbury.

Now ready, in 3 Vols., 6s. each.

WITH PORTRAIT OF THE AUTHOR, ENGRAVED ON STEEL,
BY ARMITAGE.

THE POETICAL WORKS

OF

ROBERT BUCHANAN.

NOTICES OF THIS EDITION.

"By students of poetry this collected edition will be warmly welcomed and prized."—*Nonconformist.*

"We appreciate Mr. Buchanan's power of language, which, in its Celtic suggestions of the awful and immense, in its vagueness of splendour and passion, often reaches the effects of sublimity; we can feel the tenderness of his sympathy with the human destiny, and the pathos of his trust in that unseen beneficence of which his poetry, though it has been unjustly termed a 'philosophy of rebellion,' is the reverential vindication. . . . Perhaps nothing could better bring out the distinctive character of Mr. Buchanan's poetry than a comparison of this passage with a stanza in Wordsworth's 'Ode on Immortality,' beginning, 'Earth fills her lap with pleasures of her own.' . . . All this is conceived with a grandeur, and executed with a sustained vigour, which prove that if Mr. Buchanan dreads the effacement of the Celt in the Greek, he yet cannot always divest himself of a perhaps unconscious kinship with Æschylus."—*Saturday Review.*

"There is no resisting his hold upon us as, line by line, he reveals to us, with penetrating sympathy, the deep heart's suffering of some poor victim of personal cruelty, or social neglect, or pitiless world-forces. He enters the most obscure recesses of the tangled minds and strangely pained hearts of such subjects as 'Meg Blane' and 'Nell,' with wonderful imaginative power, and lays bare the story of their lives with most fascinating art. This championship of wronged, bruised, down-trodden lives is the animating spirit of Mr. Buchanan's best work. It directs his choice of subjects as much in classical mythology as in London streets, or on the Scottish coast; wherever he goes he is drawn, as by natural affinity, towards unregarded sufferings, and the heart-eating sense of injustice and oppression. The highest testimony to Mr. Buchanan's power is that his tales of despised and oppressed lives fascinate us and win our admiration, even when we are filled with hostility to his narrow dogmatism in other directions."—*Examiner.*

"'He is a true poet, and liable to scatter some pearl of purest ray serene on any page. He is a poet, too, of most various imagination. Where could be found a stronger contrast than between the dramatic simplicity and the carefully studied faithfulness of his 'London Poems,' and the weird supernaturalness and ghostly gloom of the 'Ballad of Judas Iscariot'? He has a gift for landscape painting, second only to his rare power in the dramatic presentation of human character and emotion.'"—*New York Tribune*.

"Buchanan ist einer der bedeutendsten unter den jüngeren englischen Lyrikern . . . Während durch seine schottischen Lieder die Bäche murmeln und die Vögel schlagen, ist die Staffage der 'London Poems' die wahle russige Stadt, und mit grosser Feinheit begreift Buchanan die Menschen, denen, so zu sagen, die Himmel niemals geblaut hat und denen das Grün des Feldes eine ungeahnte Farbe ist. Die Sprache ist den Stoffeo angemessen : ernst und kräftig ; wir vermissen Ténnyson's schwellende Rundung nicht ; auch zerfallen Buchanan's Verse nicht, wie die Browning's, in verunglückte Prosa . . . Das Frauengemuth zu ergründen und ihm nachzuführen versteht Buchanan wie Wenige."—*Die Wage (Berlin)*.

"Nor has this voice of dumb, wistful yearning in man towards something higher,—of yearning such as the brute creation seemed to show in the Greek period towards the human,—found as yet any interpreter equal to Mr. Buchanan. . . To our minds, after long knowledge of these poems, they seem to us nearly perfect of their kind, realistic and idealistic alike in the highest sense . . . But these poems of Mr. Buchanan are so well known, that we need not give any example of their beauties. We are sure that he has still much— and perhaps his best work—to give us. Let us hope that his latest poems will include the richest and most genial, as well as the most powerful, of his productions."—*Spectator*.

"Except by a clique, the merit of Mr. Buchanan's poetry is generally acknowledged. . . . Let these persons be more tolerant of other tastes ; let them cease to suppose that they in their studios or clubs are mouthpieces of what is soundest and most enduring in the heart of this nation. . . . Notable in this author's work are its artistic totality and clearness of outline ; also the racy, nervous, direct, Anglo-Saxon strength of its language, for which we must go back to Byron, Wordsworth, Pope, and Chaucer. . . . The 'Art pour Art' school will say that a poet has no business to teach even by implication, to have or express any moral convictions ! What do they make of Shelley, and Dante? . . . One of our foremost living poets, and destined to become (directly or indirectly) one of our most influential."—*Gentleman's Magazine*.

"He has studied deeply at many imaginative springs, but his own well of song is unmixed with their waters. His utterance is growing clearer and more distinct every year. But in addition to this originality, there is the merit of endeavouring to assist in the formation of a superior school of poetry to that which attracts singers of a lower order. . . . In the great power then of appealing to universal humanity lies Mr. Buchanan's security. The light of Nature has been his guide, and the human heart his study. With these still as his greatest incentives he must unquestionably attain an exalted position among the poets of the nineteenth century, and produce works which cannot fail to be accepted as incontestably great, and worthy of the world's reservation."—*Contemporary Review*.

LONDON : HENRY S. KING & CO.

Now ready at all libraries, in 3 vols.,

THE THIRD EDITION

OF

THE SHADOW OF THE SWORD:

A Romance.

By ROBERT BUCHANAN.

SOME OPINIONS OF THE PRESS.

" The ' Shadow of the Sword ' is a prose poem in idea as well as expression, a wistful appeal to the Prince of Peace, who seemed still to sleep in His tomb in the garden and delay His coming . . . The main conception of Mr. Buchanan's poem is novel, in the opposition of indignant and resolute reason to this iron will and its crushing machinery. The scenes are laid in the wilder districts of ' La Bretayne Bretonnante.' A simple fisherman, Rohan Gwenfern, refuses to obey the behests of the tyrant. Partly enlightened by the teachings of an erratic missionary, who escapes the consequences of his opinions by passing with the people for half-mad, Rohan has long been cherishing a profound resentment against this system that is bereaving all the households about him. . . It is the central conception of Rohan Gwenfern that makes the book a poem rather than a novel. The novel, as we understand it, professes to reproduce actual life, without indulging too far in ideal possibilities. Now Rohan Gwenfern is legitimate and even admirable as an ideal creation. . . . We may give the highest praise to the rest of the book in point both of scenery and characters. . . . Next to his fisherman hero, Mr. Buchanan, as is fitting, has bestowed most pains on the portraiture of the Emperor. Not that, except on rare occasions, we ever see the deity of battle very near. For the most part he hovers on the lurid horizon of the story, as the giant Providence that casts the shadow of the sword, and we have vaguely to imagine the shape and features through the smoke and bloody haze of the battle-field. . . . Buonaparte was the incarnation of the war spirit in the most baneful shape of a deliberate frenzy ; nor is Mr. Buchanan by any means sparing of the eloquence of unmeasured denunciation. Yet the romantic soul of the poet cannot always resist the spell of the hero, criminal and even base as the hero may have often been. So he makes the itinerant preacher, Arfoll, involuntarily submit to that ascendancy in a pathetic description he gives of the *adieux* of Fontainebleau[1] . . . The story is told with force and fire ; and if you open it at random, after having read it through, there is scarcely a chapter that will not repay a second perusal."—*The Times.*

" The production of a first prose romance by Mr. Robert Buchanan is a literary event of some consequence. He has called the ' Shadow of the Sword ' a romance, and rightly, for his incidents and his hero are intentionally idealised out of the region of plain prose. . . . As a whole, there are few more fascinating romances, even in history itself, than the single-handed struggle of the obscure Breton peasant, Rohan Gwenfern, against the whole Napoleonic idea: its armies, its prestige, its victories, its glory, the fanaticism of all France, and the personality of the Emperor, which Mr. Buchanan represents as the deepest and widest influence of all. . . . It is in effect a tragedy after the Greek, where omnipotent destiny is one hero and one helpless man the other. . . . In our opinion, nothing in the whole novel is equal in charm to its introduction—the opening love scene between Rohan and Marcelle: an exquisite poem in itself, which draws a bitter pathos from the tragedy, which we know is to overshadow all before long. Mr. Buchanan probably, and with good cause, stakes his novel upon the struggle of one lonely, hunted man on an island of nightmares, with his whole world against him. . . . Even artistic faults cannot destroy the splendid effect of his conception as a whole, and of the manner in which he has developed it. To repeat with greater emphasis what we have already said, the ' Shadow of the Sword ' is a book to extort admiration and to fascinate the most critical readers."—*The Globe.*

"Without being told that the leading character in this strange story is taken from life, and that many of the extraordinary incidents related in it actually occurred as described, we might almost have imagined such to be the case from the extraordinary realism of the narrative. The story is told with extraordinary force and vigour, and gains a wonderful hold upon the imagination of the reader, and it is powerfully aided by the rugged picturesqueness of its whole surroundings. . . . In nothing does Mr. Buchanan show more skill than in his portrayal of the glamour which surrounded the very name of Napoleon. . . . The record of Rohan's hunted life in the cave of St. Gildas is given with great power, and the death of the poor goat Yannedik, a better Christian than many of those of the two-legged kind, is almost too pathetic. . . . The affair of the inundation is really grand. Nothing can be sweeter, too, than the character of Marcelle. . . . The book is full of pictures of extraordinary force and beauty ; the writer, thoroughly imbued with his subject, touches it at once with the skill of the poet and of the painter, and his book will be read and read again and again by all who can recognize and appreciate a true insight into and communion with the mysteries of man and of nature, joined to a power of description which it is given to few indeed to possess."—*Morning Post.*

"A Quaker does not seem, at first sight, a very likely hero for a poetical romance, and yet Mr. Robert Buchanan has made an interesting and curious story out of the adventures of his Rohan Gwenfern. . . . Here we have a struggle against society, a hopeless struggle of one man, at least as desperate as any of the colossal conflicts in M. Hugo's romances. Rohan is much more than the mere hater of war and tyranny ; he has all the Celt's delight in solitude and in the sea ; all the Celt's perverse courage on the side of forlorn and impossible causes ; much of the Celt's visionary quality."—*Pall Mall Gazette.*

"Mr. Buchanan is a poet, and this romance may be to some extent regarded as a prose poem. The pictures with which the story abounds are bright with the fancy that finds its most natural expression in verse ; the colouring is that of a poetical artist, and the weird-like imagination which throws its lurid light upon one page, and the blackness of a great cloud upon another, is that of a man who has seen visions and dreamt dreams. . . . Mr. Buchanan is never so impressive, and never carries the reader along with him so readily, as when he feels the salt spray upon his cheeks, and hears the thunder of the waves, as they burst upon the cliffs, or rush into secret caverns. The charm of the romance before us is due, we think, mainly to the profound love of nature which pervades it. . . . This bare outline may induce our readers to turn to its pages. They will not be disappointed, if they are willing for a season to exchange the realism of modern fiction for the poetical conceptions, the exciting incidents, the strong passions, and glowing fancy that belong to high romance."—*Spectator.*

"Mr. Robert Buchanan has made an exceedingly important contribution to recent literature in the 'Shadow of the Sword.' . . . The character of Rohan Gwenfern is most powerfully and consistently drawn. A hater of war at a time when martial glory was the vital essence of a Frenchman, loathing Napoleon when by the common people he was looked up to as more than saint, he refuses to present himself for conscription, and flees for his life from cave to cave of the rocks. It is artistically described how even then he cannot escape from the shedding of blood, of which he has such a horror, and the memory of this, in conjunction with his privations extending over many months, reduces him, when at last his wanderings are over and peace comes to France with the detention of the Emperor at St. Helena, almost to the level of a harmless madman. Quite as graphically drawn is the patient tenderness of Marcelle. . . . Best of all is Uncle Ewen, in whom breathed all the spirit of the Old Guard, and to whom a belief in the 'Little Corporal' was almost life. . . . The report of the victory of Ligny is the last news that reaches him, and he dies with a shout of '*Vive l'Empereur*' on his lips. . . . The story is full of dramatic points."—*Academy.*

"The finest descriptive writing of which any English writer is capable. . . . A romance pervaded by a certain atmosphere of weird and elevating meaning and purpose. This, however, is not inconsistent with the revelation of real types of character, which are brought out all the more powerfully by the background of mystic suggestion on which they move. . . . A semi-mystical, symbolic, or romantic medium, charged with weird and visionary hints of the tragical powers that lie sealed in trivial events and in trivial persons as affecting the larger movements of human destiny. . . . In a word, Mr. Buchanan has given us a romantic Epic of the Napoleonic period. It was a bold and a trying theme; but he has adequately treated it, and has worked it up to a close truly grand and touching."—*Nonconformist.*

"Mr. Buchanan has essayed in this novel a task that strikingly proves, and partially justifies, his belief in his own powers. Rohan Gwenfern is a coward, a deserter, and a murderer. It is Mr. Buchanan's thesis to show that he is a 'hero and a martyr.' The panic-stricken cur, when drawn for the conscription, is paralysed with fear. Yet his terror, which has in it nothing that is not merely selfish and base, suffices, as Mr. Buchanan would have us believe, to be the instrument of the downfall of the great Napoleon, and to make the dead Christ rise from his grave. . . . We are bound to say that the key-note of power struck in the verses which serve as a prologue to the prose, is on the whole, maintained throughout."—*World.*

"The study of a conflict between anarchy represented by individual despotism; and individual conscience in revolt. . . . Herein is set forth the struggle between a human soul morbidly sensitive to the responsibility of shedding blood and the soul of a man who looked on hecatombs of slain as no more than necessary landmarks to the limits of his own sovereignty or the sovereignty of the people whom he governed. The author does not regard the question in a narrow light, but in the full and open day of the Christian principle of charity. . . . In the 'Shadow of the Sword' it is possible to bring both the victim and the wielder before a judge; and both are confronted, a trial proceeds, and an informal verdict is recorded. Thus, we venture to think that Mr. Buchanan has done a good deal more than he claims, and that his book is not merely a subjective examination of the Shadow, but moreover an objective denouncement of the Sword. . . . From what we have said, it must not be for a moment supposed that Mr. Buchanan's romance is a dry, political essay. On the contrary, it is excessively picturesque and powerfully dramatic. The characters are not idle phantoms, but substantial facts; the style is perspicacious, vigorous, and, as a poet's style should be, full of marvellously chosen epithets—reading it is like galloping over fields of flowers."—*Yorick.*

"We cannot help wishing that the sweet, sad story of Rohan Gwenfern had been told in verse; yet even verse could hardly have been sweeter than the delicately cadenced prose in which it is written. . . . Could the prettiest of rhymed stanzas be much prettier than that in which we are told how the two cousins first discovered that their love was not that of brother and sister? We are no blind admirers of the author of the 'Shadow of the Sword;' but we are bound to say that in these volumes he has taught a lesson to his brother, and above all to his sister, novelists, which we wish they would learn. The lesson is, that nothing is more pure and modest than a really strong passion."—*Standard.*

"A work, we think, that no one but a poet could have written. Its strength and attraction lie in the depth of the author's feeling for nature, especially for nature in her wilder and weirder aspects, as she shows herself in 'the melancholy ocean,' and the awful cliffs and gloomy caverns of a stormy and solitary coast. Mr. Buchanan undoubtedly possesses in a high degree the Celtic turn for what Mr. Matthew Arnold terms 'natural magic,' the turn for 'catching and rendering the charm of nature in a wonderfully new and vivid way.' The scene of the story is laid at Kromlaix, 'in the loneliest and saddest corner of the Breton coast,' and the sea and the crags form an abiding background to the picture here shown to us which we are never allowed to lose sight of for long together. . . . A really fine and powerful romance, to whose many beauties in the way of picturesque description we regret our space will not allow us to do justice."—*Graphic.*

"Mr. Buchanan has woven a weird and striking romance out of materials that seemed too painful, and concerning a period that one might fancy was as yet too near for completely successful treatment after the manner he has adopted. . . . No hasty summary can give any idea of the depth of meaning and the power of this book. Mr. Buchanan has managed, with the utmost skill, to maintain romantic colour and charm, by the place which he gives to legend, and by the fine appreciation he shows for the fanciful and superstitious character of the people, and yet many of his portraitures are as real as though there were no element of romance in the story. The humour and the un-affected pathos of some parts is in our opinion simply masterly. Throughout the book abounds in powerful picturesque passages, is full of weird romantic touches, presents character with great force and truth, and may be regarded as a most successful experiment in a field which has not been much, if at all, ventured upon in this country."—*British Quarterly Review.*

"Whether we want learned novels or not, we have not far to look for the works of authors whose culture abundantly shows itself through their writing. Mr. Robert Buchanan has a field to himself. It is surely a matter for con-gratulation that a writer of his mark ventures into the territory of fiction at all."—*Contemporary Review.*

A FOURTH AND CHEAPER EDITION, WITH A NEW PREFACE,
IN PREPARATION.
